The Sales Executive Handbook

8 Essential Elements of Sales Management

Early Reviews of
The Sales Executive Handbook

"Thank you...[it's]:
- ***Comprehensive*** *– the chapters cover everything I would expect – awesome detail*
- ***Logical*** *in the organization of the chapters – excellent flow*
- ***Well written*** *– you speak from experience and with authority"*

> – Craig Geiger, 30-year sales professional, consumer packaged goods industry

"I'm impressed with this well-organized and comprehensive guide on how to build and manage a successful sales organization."

> – Tom Agoston, sales and marketing executive, tech sector

"Great read and this will especially be a great reference."

> – Adam Johnson, VP Sales, logistics industry

"I loved it! You cover so much, in an easy-to-read style."

> – Carol Wallace, senior executive, public relations, tech sector

"This [book] you have written is excellent!"

> – Alan Booth, executive coach

The
Sales Executive
Handbook

8 Essential Elements of
Sales Management

David P. Wallace

NOTE TO READERS

In some cases, people or companies presented in this book are based on the author's experiences. They are examples that illustrate situations. All the names have been anonymized and are not intended to represent a particular person or organization.

ISBN 978-1-7359836-0-8 (paperback)

ISBN 978-1-7359836-1-5 (ebook)

To my wife, Marianne.

She has supported and encouraged me for the last 30+ years.

I'm lucky to have found the perfect person to love.

And, even luckier still, that she loves me.

Table of Contents

Introduction

*"Our plan is to invent some sort of doohickey
that everyone wants to buy."*

— *"Visionary" in Dilbert*

As a business leader, you've worked hard to build your business. You've developed a successful product or service and have an established base of customers. Now, you're ready for growth. What's next? How do you expand your markets and grow your customer base while generating consistent, double-digit revenue increases and hitting your profitability targets? A key to your success is building a superior, high-functioning sales organization led by an effective sales manager or sales executive.

Over my 30+ years in sales and sales management, I've observed a consistent pattern when working with growing companies. CEOs, often with extensive finance or operations experience, tend to promote their top sales producer to lead their sales organization. The rationale is nearly always the same. "My top producer knows how to sell. I'll put him or her in charge so they can lead the sales team to sell like they sell." Generally, the results are not what they expected. If you've had this experience, you know what I mean and you know how hard it can be to replace that less than effective sales executive.

Effective sales management is not the same as effective selling. Effective sales executives employ a quite different set of tools than those they used as top sales producers. There are three major differences. First, a sales executive drives positive sales results from an entire sales team comprised of individuals with a wide range of talent, skills, abilities and drive. The top sales producer only needs to drive himself or herself. To generate increased sales and meet profitability goals, the sales executive coaches everyone on the sales team and orchestrates many different levels of performance, not just his or her own performance.

Second, the sales executive develops and implements the companywide sales strategy, which accounts for selling situations in a variety of geographies, industries and customer sets. It includes positioning the company's products and services against competitors and changing market conditions. The top sales producer, on the other hand, focuses on a much more limited customer set. Rather than having each sales rep create a strategy from scratch, the sales executive develops an overall strategy and helps each rep apply it to their territory.

Third, the sales executive determines which tools to make available to the entire team. The sales executive anticipates a wide range of situations and makes sure the right tools are available to meet these situations. Top sales producers effectively use the sales tools made available to them. These include customer relationship management (CRM) systems, sales brochures and collateral, market intelligence, and sales programs. They pick and choose the tools that work best for them or that they're most comfortable with.

I've written *The Sales Executive Handbook* to help business leaders choose the right sales executive and build a high-functioning sales organization. This book will be a valuable resource for anyone — founder, business owner, CEO, president or vice president of sales — who needs to make their sales organization more effective.

This Book Is Not About Sales Skills

Many business leaders have asked me: What's the best "selling skills" model? Selling skills are critical to your sales organization's success, but this book is not about selling skills. If that's what you need, there are many other books available today that present excellent sales methodologies. These books advocate various selling "styles" with names like relationship selling, solution selling, challenger sales, collaborative selling, SNAP Selling and SPIN selling. These sales styles address particular situations. They focus on specific skills that sales representatives need to develop and employ to increase their success. Often, the selling styles focus on specific stages of the sales cycle such as gauging interest, qualification, needs analysis or closing.

There are also many training companies you can hire to teach your sales reps the "skills" they need to sell, mine included. Some focus on specific skills such as qualifying opportunities, developing rapport or initiating a trial close. Others teach selling styles or methodologies. Miller-Heiman (now MHI Global), Sandler Sales and Ziglar are some of the more well-known programs. All of them teach important skills and use a variety of delivery methods such as online streaming, one-day motivational seminars, week-long workshops and ongoing coaching. Many employ a combination of these methods.

This Book Is About Building and Managing a Sales Organization

This book focuses on how to build a sales organization. It offers a structured approach to managing your company's sales function. It's a streamlined, integrated system that can be implemented whether you envision having a small sales team of 1 to 5 sales representatives or a larger sales team.

Sales management goes well beyond managing your salespeople. Effective sales management involves putting the right systems and processes in place to ensure your salespeople do the right things, at the right time, to generate the right results. It depends on creating and communicating a sales strategy that supports achievement of your overall company strategy. An effective sales executive also puts tools in place — territory plans and reviews, a customer relationship management (CRM) system, and proposal templates and training programs — to help the sales team to be effective.

By reading this book, you'll learn the eight essential elements you need to build and manage a sales organization that helps your reps sell effectively and efficiently to your market and drive revenue. The eight elements are pieces of a dynamic puzzle. All the pieces need to fit together, but the shapes change as the competitive environment changes. Following this Introduction, the book is divided into eight sections, with one section for each element. Each element starts with a short overview followed by an example highlighting the importance of addressing that element. These examples are based on companies I've worked with. All names of companies and individuals have been anonymized.

If you're just getting started with building your sales organization, I recommend reading the entire book. If your sales organization is established, you may choose to focus on specific elements. This book is written so that you can refer to the elements of greatest interest to you.

Here's an overview of the eight essential elements of sales management.

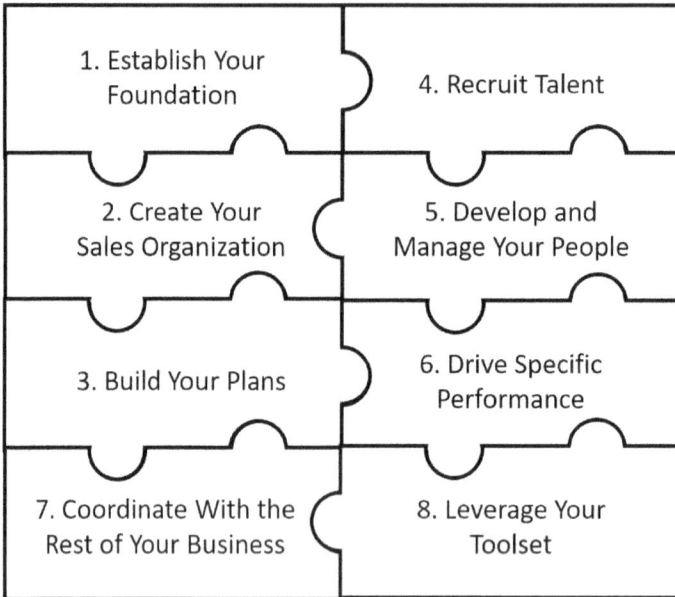

1. Establish Your Foundation	4. Recruit Talent
2. Create Your Sales Organization	5. Develop and Manage Your People
3. Build Your Plans	6. Drive Specific Performance
7. Coordinate With the Rest of Your Business	8. Leverage Your Toolset

Element 1: Establish Your Foundation

The first element is to establish your foundation. The foundation has three parts: goals, strategy and metrics. First, define goals for all levels of your organization — company, sales team, territories, key accounts and individual sales reps. Company goals are often set by the executive leadership team with the sales portion assigned to the sales team; however, they then flow down throughout the sales organization. If you don't have multiple levels in your organization, that's okay. The concept still applies; set goals and communicate them clearly to your team.

It's important to set revenue goals for the sales teams and key accounts. The most successful sales leaders also set goals for other measures that are important to their company's success. Some of these may include:

- **Product or service goals** – Selling specific product volumes or achieving certain service levels

- **Business development goals** – Opening new customers

- **Market penetration goals** – Expanding market share in specific geographies, industries or markets

Second, once you set your goals, define your strategy. Your strategy is your roadmap or path to achieving your goals. It addresses six fundamental questions, basically the where, who, what, when, how and why of sales.

Third, put metrics in place to measure success or failure. Tying the metrics to your goals will help you measure how efficiently your company is working to execute its strategy.

Element 2: Create Your Sales Organization

In many companies, especially ones that go through a period of high growth, the sales organization is created without planning or forethought. Early on, the founder or business owner does all the selling. Later, the founder hires some salespeople and promotes the best one to be the manager. Through an evolutionary process, the sales organization changes to address immediate needs. Sometimes, this evolution creates an effective team that meets the needs of both the market and the company. Often, however, evolutionary change creates dysfunction. Different groups within the sales organization compete, have conflicting goals, or simply do not support each other as they pursue their own agendas.

The most effective sales organizations are designed to address specific markets and needs. Customer-facing sales representatives receive support from back-office teams whose responsibility is to provide the sales reps with everything they need to stay in front of customers and move the sales opportunities along the sales cycle toward closing the sale. Effective sales executives have a vision and a plan for growing their sales team so it can scale up as the company grows and the associated demands of the market increase.

Element 3: Build Your Plans

Once you establish your goals, strategy, metrics and set up the sales organization, you need a plan that defines how you will execute your strategy. Basically — how will you sell to the market? For the sales team, this involves developing plans — by territory and by account — that identify specific opportunities, tactics, actions and time frames that will be used to help them achieve their goals. These plans define how individual sales reps will sell to their markets, considering local market conditions, competitive positions and customer requirements.

I highly recommend that customer-facing sales reps develop their own territory and account plans, so they own them and have confidence in them. Taken together, the individual territory plans form your overall company plan. If your business has already grown to multiple regions or business units, then the individual territory plans should roll up to form the basis of regional plans. Regional plans then roll up to the business unit level and business unit plans roll up to company plans. Through this "roll up" process, your sales executive can actively track progress to ensure company goals are addressed and achievable.

In addition to creating initial plans, effective sales executives review the plans and their sales team's progress against their plans on a regular basis. Effective sales executives review their territory and account plans at least quarterly. Plans may require more frequent review if market conditions change or if the sales representative or territory is relatively new. Territory reviews prove an excellent time to accomplish three things: 1) update plans to reflect changes in the territory, 2) better understand the local conditions that make up the broader market and 3) review metrics to track progress against goals.

Element 4: Recruit Talent

Hiring a sales team sounds so easy. Right? You just look for charismatic, charming, articulate and outgoing people who will persistently and non-offensively deliver your value proposition to qualified prospects. But, what about the quiet people? They're good at listening, an important skill for sales reps. In addition to good listeners, it's best to recruit new salespeople who are experts in your field and who write well, speak well and will represent your company professionally. They also need to demonstrate evidence of strong selling skills including the ability to uncover opportunities, qualify them and nurture prospects until they are ready to buy. Beyond actually closing deals, your sales rep candidates also need to know how to pay attention to detail, enter timely information into a CRM system, submit expenses on time and stay within budget.

Come to think of it, hiring an effective sales team may not be so easy!

Effective sales executives make a plan for hiring the sales team. They identify the roles to fill such as account manager, new business development representative, field sales, inside sales, direct sales and indirect sales. Element 2: Create Your Sales Organization covers these roles in detail. For each role, they define the temperament and skills needed: hunter versus farmer, leader versus follower, thinker versus doer, big picture strategist versus detail-oriented tactician. Finally, when selecting candidates, effective sales executives assess the trade-offs associated with experience, salary, and onboarding or training costs. Are you prepared to pay a higher salary to attract and hire an experienced sales representative? Or, will you pay less for a less-experienced sales rep but invest the money you save in training them?

Element 5: Develop and Manage Your People

It's not enough to simply hire good sales reps. You need to develop and manage them to ensure they are working toward your goals and executing your strategy. Left to their own devices, even the best sales reps will put their own interests first, which may, or may not, coincide with your strategic goals. You may need to train your sales reps. Training is essential for new sales reps — skills training, product training and company training. However, you also need to provide ongoing training to your experienced sales reps. As markets, products, techniques and customers change, your sales reps need to update their skills, outlook and abilities. That requires training. The most effective sales executives continually train their sales teams and use outside trainers when appropriate.

Performance planning is the vehicle by which you manage your sales team. Effective sales executives work with each member of their sales team to develop, implement and review tailored performance plans. Performance plans help the sales executive communicate goals and expectations, identify strengths and weaknesses, and put action steps in place to improve the effectiveness of the sales team member. Performance plans also include metrics that measure both performance and progress toward goals. They become the platform by which sales executives manage their teams.

Element 6: Drive Specific Performance

Effective sales executives understand how to use motivation, both intrinsic and extrinsic, to drive results. They lead their sales team to achieve higher performance levels, often employing three tactics: clear communication of expectations and strategy, incentive compensation and non-monetary incentive programs.

Clear communications are important to driving higher performance because sales reps are competitive by nature. If you clearly identify a goal and lay out a strategy or path to the goal, your sales reps will work hard to achieve your goals and more. If your sales reps do not know or understand what is expected of them, or if they do not know what goals you are trying to achieve, they will flounder or work toward their own goals (whether they coincide with the company's goals or not).

Many, if not most, sales reps are driven by compensation. They want to earn a lot of money and they use money as a scorecard. Therefore, you can use incentive compensation effectively to drive your sales reps' performance in furtherance of your company's strategic goals.

It's not always necessary to use monetary compensation to drive sales rep performance. Given their competitive nature, sales reps are also driven by being recognized in front of their peers and families. Recognition can be in the form of having their name listed atop a "sales leader" board, an acknowledgment before peers at a sales meeting, or a simple plaque or trophy with their name displayed prominently in the office. I've seen more than one sales rep earning well into six figures raise their performance significantly so they could win a $25 trophy to place on their desk for all to see.

Element 7: Coordinate With the Rest of Your Business

Sales forecasts and sales results drive key business decisions in other areas of your company. Marketing relies on sales to define the criteria they use when qualifying leads. Manufacturing determines their production schedules based on forecasted sales demand. Finance manages cash flow and adherence to bank debt covenants based on forecasted collection of payments from customers.

Truly effective sales leaders work with their counterparts in all parts of the company – marketing, finance, operations, manufacturing, supply chain/procurement and human resources. Executives leading these functions all depend on accurate and timely information from sales. In turn, sales reps are also dependent on these functional areas to keep their commitments to customers. Manufacturing and supply chain control production volumes and delivery lead times. Finance ensures the company has the capital available to pay for sales growth. Increased sales demand more inventory, receivables, production and staff. All which costs money. Finance needs to plan for this growth. Based on sales forecasts, the human resources department recruits staff for other departments across the company such as production, logistics and procurement.

Without good relationships and strong communications with counterparts who lead other company functions, the sales executive will not be able to drive the revenue needed to meet your company's strategic goals.

Element 8: Leverage Your Toolset

You amass a lot of data as you build your sales organization, develop strategies and execute your plans. This data can provide valuable insights to your business if you use available tools to turn the data into usable information.

Today's sales leaders leverage the full range of tools available to them to turn data into information. These tools include customer relationship management systems (CRMs) used to track customers, contacts, opportunities, deals, products and competitors. They also include data intelligence and dashboard tools such as PowerBI, QlikView and Tableau. When these tools are tied to your company's enterprise resource planning (ERP) system or financial software, your executive team can have a 360-degree view of your sales efforts, customers, products and markets.

Now, let's get started exploring each of these eight elements in depth. Or, if you need to focus on a specific element, jump to that section.

Element 1: Establish Your Foundation

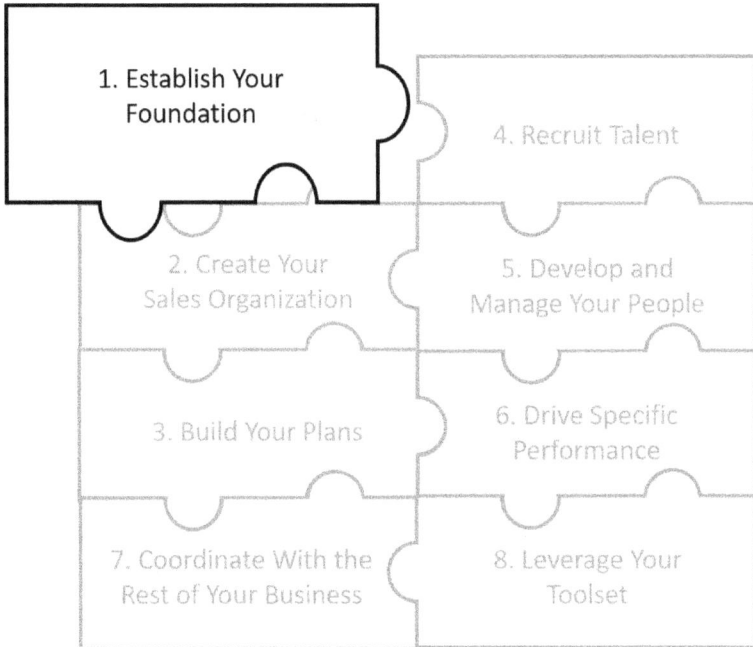

"*You must have a strong foundation if you're going to have a strong superstructure.*"

– Gordon Hinkley, religious leader, Presidential Medal of Freedom recipient

A successful business is built upon a firm foundation. Three of the most important building blocks in your foundation are 1) goals, 2) a strategy to achieve those goals and 3) metrics to track progress against the goals. Goals are important because they define where you are going. Strategy is important because it defines how you will get there. Metrics are important because they provide the tools to measure how well, or poorly, you are doing.

Goals and strategy should not be confused with your company's mission. Mission defines a higher-level purpose for the company. Mission is the reason the company is in business at all. Goals are what the company aims to accomplish within a defined time frame in pursuit of the overall mission. For example, a company's mission may be to connect the world through the best networking solutions. However, one of its goals may be to deliver $100 million of revenue through sales of 5G transceivers. The mission is higher-level; the goal is specific.

The next three chapters discuss setting goals (Chapter 1: Goals), defining a strategy to accomplish the goals (Chapter 2: Strategy) and developing metrics (Chapter 3: Metrics).

Element 1: Establish Your Foundation

Shady River Turf*

Shady River Plantings grows and sells landscape plants to garden centers and commercial landscapers. Robert James started Shady River Plantings in 1960 and ran it until he died in 2012. After he passed away, his three sons returned home to assume control of the business. When James ran Shady River, he found that through hard work and good fortune the business grew and he was able to provide well for his family. However, when his sons took over, they were challenged to generate sufficient profits and cash flow to cover the needs of their three families, their mother, and Shady River's employees, operations and debt service. The company floundered.

The James brothers brought in an outside advisor who helped them set a series of goals for themselves and for Shady River. They felt the goals were achievable, but not without a plan and effort. Next, they developed a strategy to achieve their goals. Their strategy accounted for products and services, markets and trends, financial needs and restrictions, the competitive landscape, available resources, and operational needs. In addition, they also put in place a set of metrics that would indicate on a granular level how well Shady River was progressing against its goals and performing against its strategy.

Within four years of adopting the new strategy, Shady River Plantings was meeting its goals. Today, Shady River is a major supplier of landscaping products, not just plants, to landscapers, athletic facilities, golf courses, commercial facilities and college campuses throughout the northeastern United States. They accomplished this by taking the time to establish their foundation.

*Company and individual names have been changed.

Chapter 1: Goals

"If you don't know where you are going,
you'll end up someplace else."

— *Yogi Berra, New York Yankees*

Yogi Berra, Hall-of-Fame catcher for the New York Yankees and master of the humorous turn of phrase, dropped out of school after the eighth grade, but the idea he conveyed could have come straight from an MBA management textbook. If a company does not set goals, it will not be in control of where it goes and whether it succeeds.

Set Goals

Successful businesses set goals and manage to those goals. Goals are set at the highest level and then subdivided into smaller goals assigned to groups and individuals throughout the company. The idea is that the actions of each employee are guided by the employee's individual goals. Then, all individual goals, in turn, feed the goals at the next level up in the organization and so on. A well-managed sales organization may handle its goals as shown below.

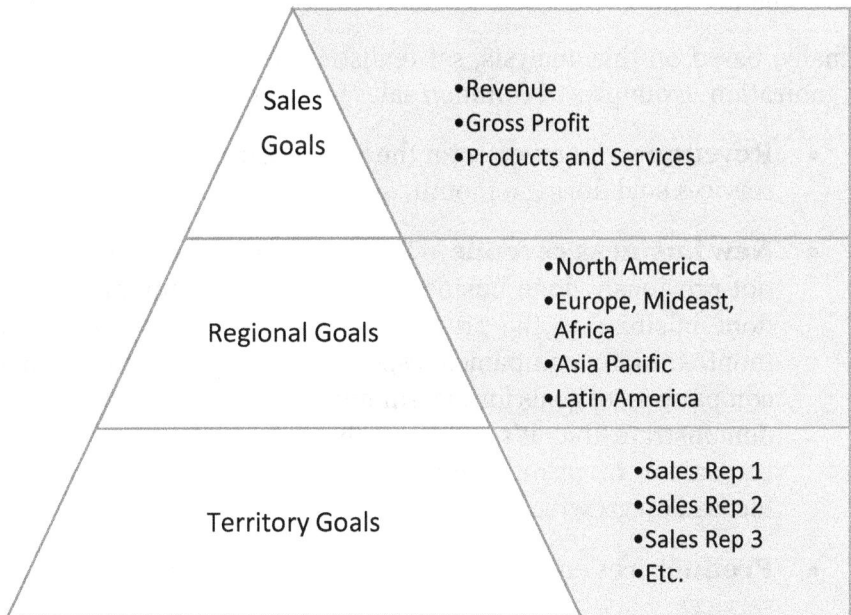

Sales Goals	• Revenue • Gross Profit • Products and Services
Regional Goals	• North America • Europe, Mideast, Africa • Asia Pacific • Latin America
Territory Goals	• Sales Rep 1 • Sales Rep 2 • Sales Rep 3 • Etc.

In the sales organization, the sales reps' territory goals (or quotas) for a region collectively contribute to achieving the regional manager's goal. All regional managers' goals, in turn, collectively contribute to the overall sales organization goal. Finally, the sales organization's goal plus goals for the other functional areas of a company, such as marketing, finance and operations, support achievement of the company's strategic goals.

Company Sales Goals

When setting your company's sales goals, look at the market first. What drives growth in each of the industries in which you sell your products? How much share does your firm have in each market? What are the competitive environments in your markets? Can you expect to increase or lose share in each of the markets?

Next, solicit input from your sales team. Ask them to identify opportunities and determine the probability of closing them. Have them project what they think the market will bear when buying your company's products and services, as well as those of your competitors. This should be an iterative process to develop a realistic market assessment.

Finally, based on this analysis, set realistic sales goals for your sales organization. Examples of common sales goals are:

- **Revenue** – Net revenue for the business from all products and services sold during a month, quarter or year.

- **New business revenue** – Revenue from customers who had not previously done business with your company or had not done business in the previous 12 months, 24 months or 36 months. Many companies, especially young, growth-oriented companies, set goals for incremental new business. These goals demonstrate that it's not enough to generate sales revenue equivalent to prior years. These goals keep the company focused on growth.

- **Product revenue** – Revenue from specific products or services.

Next, you'll want to individualize the goals, apportioning them appropriately to each sales rep and territory.

Individual Sales Goals

When I started my career at IBM as a sales representative in the 1980s, I was assigned to a major account in New York City. I shared the account with the senior sales rep who was also my mentor. Together, we were assigned a quota of about $15 million. My share of the quota as a first-year sales representative came to just under $5 million. In 1983, that was a large sum.

As large as it was, though, my $5 million goal was just a tiny piece of IBM's overall sales goal. My goal was part of the larger account goal of $15 million. Our account goal fed into our manager's goal of $30 million. And, his goal fed the account executive's goal of $60 million. The account executive' goal fed the branch manager's goal of over $100 million. Continuing, the branch manager's goal fed the regional manager's goal which fed the area manager's goal.

In all, there were about nine sales levels within IBM, each with its own goal. By the time all the goals were rolled up, IBM's corporate sales goal in 1983 was about $40 billion.

At that time, IBM was one of the world's most successful and most admired sales organizations. One of the keys to its success was setting clear goals and cascading them down through the company. Goals were assigned to each division, region, territory, account and sales representative.

I had my own goals. Each of my peers had their own goals. We knew what our goals were. We knew what was expected of us. We owned our goals and were determined to succeed. Our goals were personal. No matter what size your company is, all sales goals need to be broken down to the individual level.

Expand to Non-Revenue Sales Goals

As shown in the IBM example, sales goals are often defined as revenue goals. However, to be most successful, your company's sales goals should encompass a wider range of goals including non-revenue sales goals. These goals are best linked to the sales strategy and the company's overall goals.

Here are some examples of non-revenue sales goals. You can choose those that support your sales strategy:

- **Margin** – Gross margin or net margin are commonly set as goals, particularly in the financial services market or in businesses where the sales representatives have greater leeway in negotiating prices with customers.

- **Products and services** – These goals might be used to drive sales of products that are strategic to your company's success. These may be new products, which are more difficult to sell. Or, you may set a goal to sell more products that have a higher margin or are critical to your entry into a new market.

- **Product mix** – You may assign a goal to achieve a desired product mix such as 80% of revenue from product A and 20% from product B. Alternatively, goals can be expressed in terms of unit volume rather than revenue.

- **New customers** – It's easier to generate new revenue from existing customers than from new customers. But to grow, you need to set goals for growth in the number of new customers or active customers. These types of goals signal to sales reps that the company must grow its customer base to succeed.

- **Customer satisfaction** – This measure is more often used as a metric to measure progress toward achieving other goals such as market expansion or low customer turnover rate. However, sometimes it is defined as a goal in its own right. Customer satisfaction goals are usually defined as a percentage of "satisfied" or "well-satisfied" customers, as measured by customer surveys. Net Promoter Scores (NPS) also measure customer satisfaction. Today, it's easy to conduct customer surveys using online tools such as Google Forms or Survey Monkey.

- **Market share/market penetration** – These goals are more difficult to apply at the individual contributor level. But it is possible to set these goals, especially if the market is large, there are few competitors and current share/penetration is low:

    - *Industry* – Used most often to penetrate an adjacent or related industry (e.g., moving from residential construction to commercial construction).

    - *Geography* – Used when a company is expanding its geographic footprint (e.g., from the Northeast U.S. to the Southern states or Midwest).

    - *Demographics* – Used to attract customers that have a different profile from current customers (e.g., sell to middle-market companies versus large corporations).

SMART Goals, CLEAR Goals

When setting goals for yourself and your company, there are two well-known acronyms you can use: SMART goals and CLEAR goals. Both work well. George T. Doran coined the term SMART goal in 1981 when he was the Director of Corporate Planning for Washington Water Power Company. SMART is an acronym for Specific, Measurable, Assignable, Realistic and Time-bound. Each one of the five SMART components is critical. If any one component is missing from the goal, you will be unlikely to reach your goal or you will not know when you've reached it:

- **Specific** – The goal must be clear and unambiguous.

- **Measurable** – Results must be measurable in some way (e.g., number of products sold each week or percent of goal completed).

- **Assignable** – The goal must specify who will do it.

- **Realistic** – The goal must state the results that can realistically be achieved given available resources.

- **Time-bound** – The goal must have a definite starting point and ending point, and a fixed duration.

An example of a SMART goal is, "By the end of this year, John Jones will grow annual sales to XYZ customer by 10% year-over-year."

In 2015, entrepreneur and Olympic gold medalist, Adam Kreek, proposed an updated version of SMART goals. He proposed CLEAR goals to reflect today's collaborative, team-oriented business environment. CLEAR stands for Collaborative, Limited, Emotional, Appreciable and Refinable.

- **Collaborative** – The goal must have a social framework so individuals work and support each other as a team.

- **Limited** – The goal must be limited in both scope and duration so that you can determine when it is completed.

- **Emotional** – The goal must make an emotional connection with employees. It should connect to their core energy and passion.

- **Appreciable** – Big goals must be broken down into smaller actions so they can be accomplished more quickly and easily for long-term gain.

- **Refinable** – Set a clearly defined goal, but as new situations or information arise, allow yourself to refine and modify the goal. Anticipate change as it will inevitably happen.

An example of a CLEAR goal to achieve the customer growth goal defined above may be to "Deliver a high-level of responsiveness to XYZ customer by engaging the product management team within 24 hours to address reported product performance issues."

Both SMART goals and CLEAR goals reflect the need for clear definition and a time horizon for achievement. They also focus on making goals realistic and achievable. Kreek, however, tries to capture the rapid, fluid nature of the current business environment where information flows can cause you to reevaluate your goals.

Whether you develop SMART goals, CLEAR goals or another acronym-based goal, make sure you are defining goals rather than dreaming dreams.

Chapter 2: Strategy

"Strategy is about making choices, trade-offs; it's about deliberately choosing to be different."

— Michael Porter, Harvard Business School

"The essence of strategy is choosing what not to do."
— Michael Porter, Harvard Business School

While goals define where you want to go, strategy says how you plan to get there.

Your sales strategy is your plan to achieve your sales goals. As management guru and Harvard Business School professor Michael Porter points out, your strategy is all about making choices that differentiate you and your offerings. Jeroen De Flander, best-selling

author on strategy execution, asks more succinctly, "What's the use of measuring speed if you don't go in the right direction?"

How to Develop a Sales Strategy

Sales goals are important for setting the destination. Equally important is the strategy for how you will get there. To develop a complete sales strategy, you need to address six questions:

• **What** will you sell?	• Your products, services and solutions
• **Where** will you sell?	• Your target market – defined by need, geography, industry, or demographics
• **Who** will you sell to?	• The decision makers and influencers – names, titles, positions, responsibilities
• **How** will you sell?	• Your route to your customers (phone sales, field sales with direct employees, agents or distributors, the internet), sales activities and marketing programs
• **When** will you sell?	• Customer needs, pain points and buying signals
• **Why** should customers buy from you?	• Your value proposition and competitive advantage

What will you sell?

What is your product, service or solution? This is a fundamental question. What do you have to offer? You must be able to describe your offering clearly and succinctly.

- **Product** — A product is typically a physical offering such as clothing, tools or automobiles. It can also be a digital offering such as software applications, data or e-books.

- **Service** — A service is work that you or your company perform for a customer. Services may include work such as bookkeeping and accounting, equipment repair or consulting.

- **Solution** — Solutions combine multiple products and services to deliver an end-to-end offering that addresses a customer's problem or need. An example of a solution is logistics support in the transportation industry. Instead of simply offering a truck or a driver, a logistics firm will provide a solution that includes trucks, drivers, planning, pickup, warehousing and delivery. The logistics solution addresses the whole problem faced by the customer, not just a part of the problem.

Where will you sell?

Where will you sell your products, services or solutions? Where is your target market?

Your target market is the set of customers and prospects who will buy your products. You may define your target market by location or geography, industry or demographic.

- **Location or geography** — Target markets based on location or geography are often used with products or solutions that are low-priced, have small margins or appeal to users in a specific geography. Snowmobiles or snowplows are examples of products whose target market is specific to geography. It wouldn't make much sense to sell these products to prospects in tropical climates. They have no snow. However, prospects in snowy climates are an ideal target market. In North America, sellers of snowmobiles and snowplows target areas such as the Rocky Mountain states, the northern plains states, New England, Canada and Alaska.

- **Industry** — Companies selling products specific to niche industries target markets based on industry. Examples of industry-based target markets may include companies selling medical x-ray machines targeting the healthcare industry or specific manufacturing companies targeting the aviation or power generation industries. In these cases, the products or solutions the sellers provide are specific to an industry and narrow in scope.

- **Demographic** — Demographic target markets are based on the demographic profiles of your ideal customers. Demographics may include size of company, spending patterns, growth rate, business-to-business or business-to-consumer, or any other set of characteristics that distinguish companies in the target market. Venture capital firms may target start-up companies experiencing very high revenue growth in new industries with young management teams. Private equity firms, on the other hand, may target middle-market companies with established management teams in unconsolidated markets (markets with many small companies). Financial advisors, wealth management companies and local insurance agencies may target successful small business owners.

Often companies will view their target market as having a combination of location, industry and demographics. Taken together, these characteristics present an "ideal customer profile." The ideal customer profile is a composite of what your best customers look like. It also defines the types of prospects you will most likely close and do business with. Your sales teams should focus their time on selling to these "ideal" prospects.

Who will you sell to?

Once you've identified the companies in your target market, you need to identify "who" it is within the target company that you need to sell to. These are the decision makers, influencers, gatekeepers and others your sales team needs to interact with to close a sale. Sometimes the "who" targets are defined by title, role or position.

For instance, if you're selling expensive tooling equipment to a manufacturing company, you may target the company president or vice president of operations. For other offerings or solutions, you may determine that you need to sell to a series of mid-level managers such as a product manager, procurement manager or finance manager. Generally, I find it's most effective to start higher up in an organization and be directed down to the right decision maker. It's easier to work down into an organization than to start at the bottom and work your way up.

Generally, you will not have a single "who" that you must sell to; there may be several decision makers and influencers. A complete strategy will identify the various individuals, titles, roles and positions that you must target to close a sale.

How will you sell?

"How will you sell?" addresses the way you will go to market. How will you structure your sales team? How will you penetrate your target markets?

- **Sales organization structure** — "How" you go to market often determines how you structure your sales organization. Your sales structure may include direct sales or indirect sales. A direct sales team is made up of both field sales reps and inside sales reps. Field sales reps work directly for your company and work out in the "field" visiting customers and prospects, engaging in face-to-face selling. Inside sales reps work "inside" your company, selling via the telephone, email, chat or other electronic methods. Inside sales reps rarely, if ever, meet customers in person, face-to-face; all interactions are done remotely. With indirect sales, you leverage channel partners such as agents or distributors. Channel partners are independent businesses, sole proprietors or larger companies that sell your product to their customers. Sales organization structure is discussed in greater depth in Element 2: Create Your Sales Organization.

- **Market penetration** — In addition to how your sales team is organized, "how will you sell" addresses the various sales activities and marketing programs needed to support your team and deliver your message to your target market. Sales activities may include conferences and trade shows, webinars, and sales "events" or "blitz weeks" where all sales reps in the company spend a few days or a week focused on selling only a single product or solution. Marketing programs can be advertising, public relations campaigns, sales support programs or a variety of other programs designed to increase company, brand or product awareness within the target market.

When will you sell?

All sales follow a sales cycle and all purchases follow a buying cycle. "When" you sell must take both the sales and buying cycles into account. The sales cycle is the steps the sales team must progress through to achieve success. The buying cycle is the steps the buyer goes through when buying a product, service or solution. As your sales team progresses along the sales cycle, they should also monitor their customer's progress along the buying cycle. Successful sales will synchronize the two cycles so that the sales reps are meeting their customer's needs at the right times.

Sales cycles differ across products, customers and selling organizations. Some have more steps, some fewer. Sometimes the sales cycle is so quick you may not even notice it. Other times, the sales cycle lasts days, weeks, months or even years. It depends on the complexity of the product, the readiness of the customer to buy and the ability of the sales team. A common sales cycle follows.

Element 1: Strategy

Sales Cycle

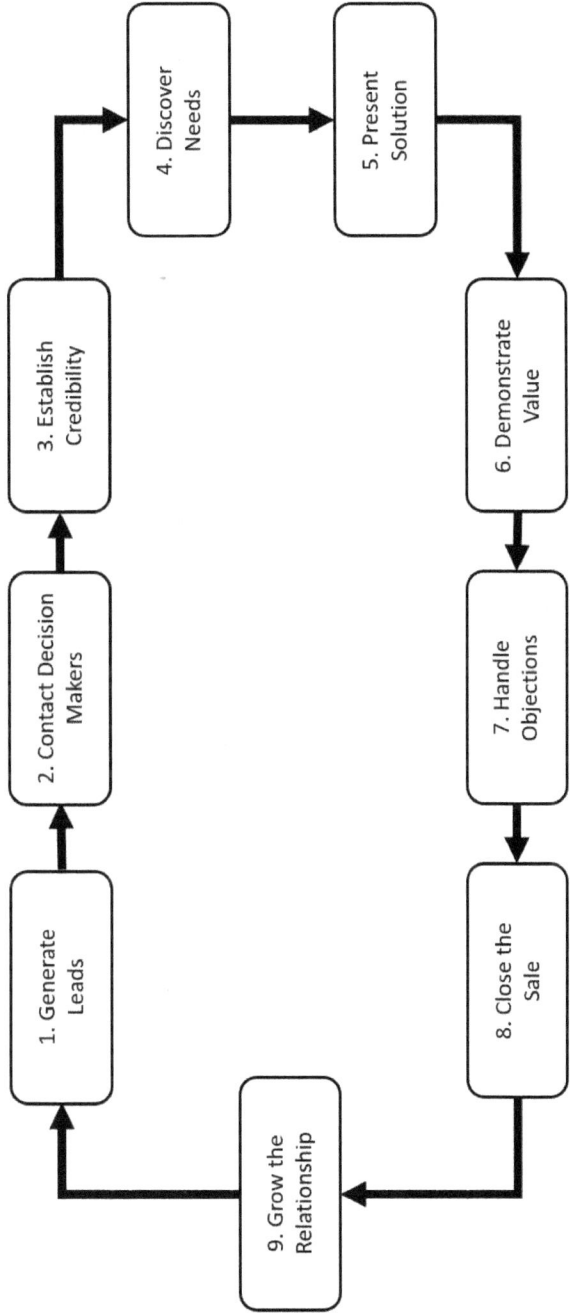

1. Generate Leads
2. Contact Decision Makers
3. Establish Credibility
4. Discover Needs
5. Present Solution
6. Demonstrate Value
7. Handle Objections
8. Close the Sale
9. Grow the Relationship

The buying cycle is related to the sales cycle. It helps answer the question: "When is a customer ready to buy?" The buying cycle is the steps the buyer goes through when buying a product, service or solution. Like the sales cycle, the buying cycle differs by product, company or buyer. It may be fast. Or, it may take a long time depending on the complexity and importance of the purchase to the buyer, the price, and the urgency of the customer's need.

As you develop your sales strategy, recognize that there will be steps that your buyer needs to go through. Anticipate these steps so that you move your buyer steadily forward through the buying cycle in the shortest time.

A common buying cycle is shown on the next page.

Why should customers buy from you?

The final question your sales strategy needs to address is "Why should customers buy your product, service or solution?" Specifically, why should they *buy from you* rather than from your competitors? It's important to clearly define your value proposition and your competitive advantage:

- **Value proposition** — The "why" is your value proposition. It differentiates your product or solution from other products and solutions available to your customers. Why should they buy your product? Do you offer better quality? More features? More appropriate features? Lower price? Longer life? Your value proposition can address one, two or several benefits for your target market.

Element 1: Strategy

Buying Cycle

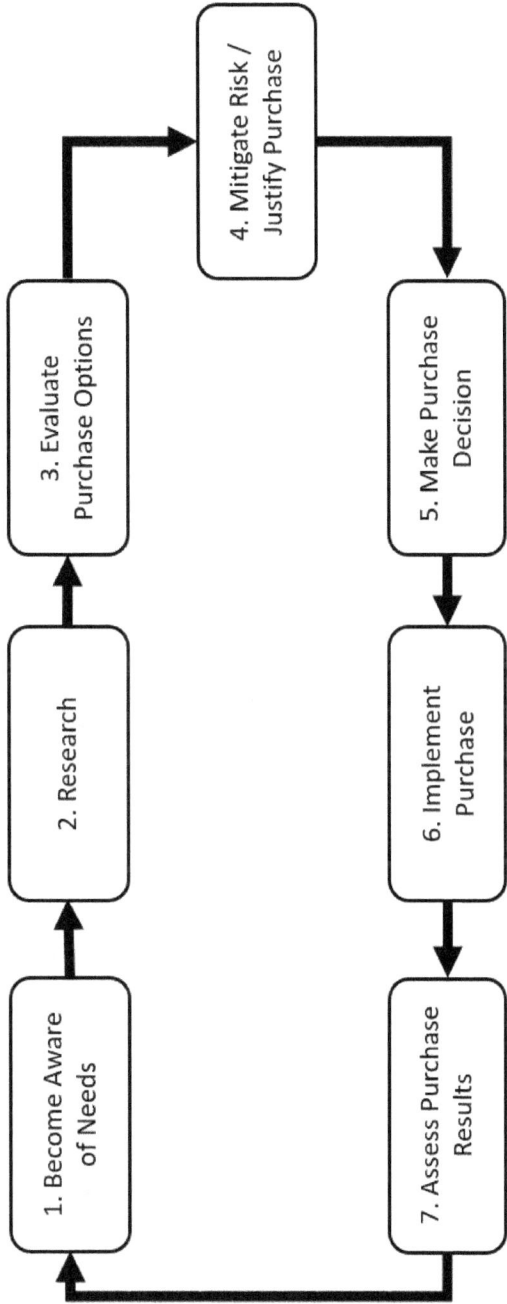

1. Become Aware of Needs

2. Research

3. Evaluate Purchase Options

4. Mitigate Risk / Justify Purchase

5. Make Purchase Decision

6. Implement Purchase

7. Assess Purchase Results

- **Competitive advantage** — The "why" is also your competitive advantage. It differentiates your company and your offering from your competition. Competitive advantages may include unique product features, purchase terms, product availability, installation, maintenance services or anything else that offers your customers greater benefit from you than they can get from your competitors.

Sales Strategy Statement

Based on your answers to these six questions, you can draft your company's sales strategy statement. A sales strategy statement is a high-level statement of how you will approach achieving your goals. A strategic plan (covered in detail in chapter 8) includes the activities, timing and accountability assignments necessary to execute on the strategy. Here's an example of a simple strategy statement for a small business:

> "Northeast Lighting delivers cost-effective, high-quality LED lighting solutions (*what*) to commercial customers with a need to illuminate an indoor or outdoor area of at least 10,000 square feet in Connecticut, Rhode Island and Massachusetts (*where*). We sell to facilities managers and chief financial officers (*who*) through both a direct sales team and channel partners such as architects and building contractors (*how*). Customers engage Northeast Lighting during the project design phase for new construction and for existing installations that are at least five years old (*when*). Customers buy from Northeast Lighting to take advantage of our competitive pricing, superior technical expertise and ability to deliver lighting solutions that provide an average of 50% more light at a fraction of their current cost with a typical payback time of 12 to 24 months (*why*)."

The following table summarizes the answers for the Northeast Lighting example. To clarify your company's strategy, use the following table to answer the six questions.

Question	Northeast Lighting Example	Your Company
What is your product, service or solution?	• Cost-effective, high-quality LED lighting solutions	
Where will you sell your products, services or solutions?	• Commercial customers with a need to illuminate an indoor or outdoor area of at least 10,000 square feet • Located in Connecticut, Rhode Island or Massachusetts	
Who will you sell to?	• Facilities managers • Chief financial officers	
How will you sell?	• Direct sales team • Channel partners such as architects and building contractors	
When will you sell?	• During the project design phase for new construction	

Question	Northeast Lighting Example	Your Company
	• Existing installations that are at least five years old	
Why should customers buy from you?	• Competitive pricing • Superior technical expertise • Ability to deliver lighting solutions that provide an average of 50% more light at a fraction of their current cost with a typical payback time of 12-24 months	

Chapter 3: Metrics

"In God we trust; all others bring data."

– W. Edwards Deming

W. Edwards Deming is best known as the statistician and management consultant who helped rebuild Japan following World War II. Deming theorized that productivity and profitability will increase when companies focus on delivering quality. In 1951, the Japanese Union of Scientists and Engineers (JUSE) established the Deming Prize to recognize individuals for their contributions to the field of Total Quality Management (TQM) and manufacturing businesses that have successfully implemented TQM. In the U.S., the Malcolm Baldrige National Quality Award (given by the President) recognizes the performance excellence of both public and private U.S. organizations.

As Deming implies with his quote above, to achieve consistently high quality, output needs to be measured. This is true in sales as well as manufacturing. Your sales team will deliver a better sales effort and better sales results when they know what you expect of them and measure their progress throughout the sales cycle.

Use Metrics to Achieve Your Company Goals

To measure a company's progress toward achieving its goals, I suggest developing some basic metrics. Metrics can also be used to measure how efficiently the company is working to execute its strategy to achieve its goals.

Goals are the endpoints of success for your company — your company's purpose. Some goals are short-term, to be accomplished within 1 to 3 years. Other goals are long-term, with a time horizon of 5, 10, or even 15 years. Metrics are the intermediate measurements that assess progress toward achieving the goals.

Here is an example that demonstrates the difference between goals and metrics. Suppose you are driving from New York to Boston.

The *goals* of the drive are:

1. Arrive in Boston

2. Arrive by a certain time, say 4:00 p.m.

The *metrics* you could use to determine if you will achieve your goal — arriving in Boston by 4:00 — could be:

1. **Fuel level** – Do you have enough gas to get to Boston?

2. **Distance** – How far have you driven since leaving New York and how far is it still to Boston?

3. **Speed** – How fast are you driving?

4. **Time** – What time is it now? How much more time will it take to get to Boston?

As you can see from the example, you may have only a few important goals. But you can use several metrics to determine if you are on the right path to achieve the goals.

As a sales executive, you may set specific goals for your sales organization. Your goals may be:

1. Achieve $25 million in revenue this year

2. Generate 50% of incremental revenue from existing customers (i.e., repeat customers)

To measure if you are on track to achieve your sales goals, you may create metrics to measure related activities and checkpoints, such as:

- **Customer satisfaction rates** – Are our customers happy with our products or solutions?

- **Sales call volume** – Are the sales representatives making enough customer calls?

- **Sales pipeline** – Do we have enough identified opportunities that our sales team is working on?

- **Forecast accuracy** – Does my sales team accurately report how much business they will bring in each month or quarter?

Tie Metrics to Goals and Targets

Metrics measure progress against goals. Therefore, you will want to tie your sales metrics to your company's sales goals. For instance, if your company has set a strategic goal of attaining $100 million of sales revenue, you will want to measure how much your sales team has sold each month over the course of the year. If your sales team has sold $30 million of revenue in the first quarter of the year and sales are not seasonal, then it appears from the sales metric that the sales team is on pace to exceed its $100 million goal. However, if they sold only $15 million during that time, then it's equally apparent that the sales team is not on pace to meet or exceed its $100 million sales goal.

Revenue run rates may not be enough to measure success, though. Using the example above, if your sales team has sold $30 million of revenue in the first quarter, but the sales pipeline is empty, then your team may not be on pace to meet its $100 million goal. Similarly, if your team has sold only $20 million in the first quarter, but the pipeline is stocked with 150% of its normal volume and the opportunities are well qualified, then you may be in an excellent position to exceed your goal.

This brings us to an important point. Select metrics that measure the factors with the greatest influence over your ultimate success in achieving your goals. For the annual revenue goal, measure revenue to date and size of the pipeline. Then, add metrics that measure the other factors contributing to building the pipeline such as number of sales calls made, proposals delivered, inbound call volume or seasonal shipments. Every business and industry will have its own factors that drive success and its own metrics to measure its progress toward success.

Use Systems to Measure and Report

After you identify the metrics essential to tracking the success factors for your business, set up the systems to measure the success factors and report the metrics. Ideally, the data used to create your metrics is gathered in the normal course of business. Sales representatives should not have to take additional actions to collect and report the data. For example, revenue data is automatically collected by finance when a product is sold. The company also collects additional information at the time of sale such as customer name, date of sale, ship-to location, industry and volume. Other sources such as industry reports and annual reports can give you access to additional data (e.g., customer size or demographics) needed for your metrics. All this data is available without the sales representative having to do anything other than sell the product and enter the sale into your order-entry or accounting system.

In addition to entering orders, I highly recommend that your sales representatives track their opportunities in a customer relationship management system (CRM). Salesforce, Zoho, HubSpot and Microsoft Dynamics CRM are some of the most used CRM systems. Like an order-entry system, a CRM system fully integrated into your company's sales process becomes a treasure trove of data to feed the metrics you need to manage your business. The most important metric available from the CRM is the sales pipeline. When your sales representatives consistently enter the sales opportunities they're working on in the CRM and maintain that information throughout the sales cycle, you'll be able to determine how much business is in the sales pipeline, by stage of the sales cycle, at any given point in time. CRM data can also be very granular, allowing you to measure pipelines by customer, product, likelihood to close and many other factors.

Other metrics regarding customers and prospects will be available to you through your CRM. A simple count of active customers and active prospects can indicate progress on growing the customer base. When combined with your order-entry or accounting system, the CRM helps measure customer order frequency and how many customers have become dormant. A dormant customer can be defined as any customer that has not placed an order in the last year or last two years, depending on your business's sales cycle or the time required to move an opportunity from lead to sale close.

Common metrics used by successful sales organizations include:

- **Revenue**
    - By month or run rate
    - By product
    - By industry
    - By sales representative
    - By sales office
    - By customer type

- **Customers**
    - New customers landed
    - Lost customers
    - Dormant customers

- **Pipeline by sales stage**
    - Revenue (weighted by the percentage likelihood to close and unweighted)
    - Product volume – Revenue and units
    - Prospects
    - Customers

- **Transactions**
  - Won/lost ratio
  - Average size
    - Revenue
    - Margin
    - Volume
  - Length of sales cycle (time to close)

This list is by no means exhaustive, but it gives you an idea of the variety of metrics you can develop and track. Your sales goals and company goals should help determine the metrics you choose.

Maintain Accountability

Setting goals and measuring progress is not enough for success. The best sales executives hold their sales teams accountable for their goals.

Most sales organizations assign a quota to each sales representative. The quota represents that portion of the overall sales goal — usually revenue, margin, new customers or some combination of these — the individual sales representative is expected to produce. Many sales organizations maintain sales representative accountability by tying the rep's compensation to their quota attainment.

You can tie compensation to performance in several ways:

- **Pay a bonus upon achieving 100% of quota** — If a sales representative earns a base salary of $100,000, the company may pay the rep an additional bonus of $25,000 if the rep meets or exceeds their assigned quota of $1 million.

- **Pay a commission percentage on the revenue generated** — In this case, the company may pay a 2.5% commission on all revenue generated by the rep. If the rep generates $1 million of revenue, the rep would earn $25,000 of commissions.

- **Pay a commission on revenue (or margin) generated and increase the commission rate for all revenue generated over quota** — In this case, the company may pay 2.5% commission on revenue up to quota ($1 million) and an additional 1% commission for all revenue generated over quota. So, if the rep generates $1.5 million of revenue against a $1 million quota, the rep's commissions would total $42,500. This is made up of $25,000 for achieving the $1 million of quota [$1 million x 2.5%] plus $17,500 for selling an additional $500,000 over quota [$500,000 x 3.5%).

Compensation tied to quota is one effective way to hold your sales teams accountable for reaching their goals. Another way is to meet regularly with your team to review their sales metrics and how each team member measures up to those metrics. Hold these review meetings with sales team members weekly (preferred) or biweekly. The lowest acceptable frequency for these meetings is monthly and that should only be in rare circumstances where the sales cycle is very long and the team is geographically dispersed.

Go Beyond Quotas, Measure Activities

Measuring attainment against quotas is a good start to achieving sales success. But you need to go further. Actions drive results. Measure the activities that drive the results you seek. If a rep isn't engaged in the activities that drive sales results, you can provide coaching. See Element 5: Managing Your People for more information on managing performance.

Several years ago, I managed a sales team that had both outside sales representatives and inside sales representatives. Our company maintained, overhauled and repaired turbines for power generation plants. The outside sales reps (aka field sales reps) conducted all face-to-face calls with customers. They gathered bid requirements, prepared proposals and closed deals. Most of the outside sales representatives were technical engineers who focused on the technical details of our solutions.

The inside sales representatives, on the other hand, rarely met customers in person. Their interactions were 8-minute phone calls. During their brief conversations, the inside sales reps spent most of their time chit-chatting and developing relationships. They learned about the customers' spouses, children and home life/work life. Calls from our inside sales representatives became brief respites for our customers from the daily demands of their work. After a few minutes of social catch up, the inside sales representatives asked key questions about the company's power plants and their turbine maintenance plans.

The inside sales representatives recorded all the information they gathered in the calls, including both personal and professional data. Our reps genuinely cared about our customers, their families, their hobbies and aspirations. Meticulous tracking of information enabled our sales team to develop relationships with decision makers and identify all relevant information about every turbine we maintained or wanted to maintain.

Our inside sales effort was critical to our sales success. Inside sales reps established relationships, developed our sales pipeline and secured invitations to bid or submit proposals. To foster success and track our progress, we measured inside sales rep activities that went well beyond revenue. By number, we tracked and measured each rep's daily phone dials, contacts made, turbine installations identified, opportunities uncovered, proposal requests received and many more activities.

In addition to tracking metrics for these key activities, we also paid our inside sales representatives on their performance against the metrics. We paid $10 for each substantive conversation, $25 for each turbine identified, $45 for each proposal and so on. Based on these measures and our reps' performance, our company developed a market database recognized as a competitive advantage in our market. We used this database to meet and exceed our company sales goals each year while giving our inside sales representatives a path to earning a significant income.

Metrics and Strategy

While metrics are used to measure a company's progress toward achieving its goals, they also provide an assessment of the company's strategy. Is it being executed properly? Is it the right strategy for successfully achieving the company's goals?

When the metrics show that the company is not making suitable progress toward meeting its goals, this does not necessarily mean that your team needs to work harder or longer. You need to assess two things:

- **Strategy execution** — Examine your team's execution of the strategic plan. Are they taking the right steps? Have they properly identified and targeted the markets and customers identified in the strategy? Are they using the right channels to reach their markets? Are they positioning and selling the right products or mix? A strategy may be valid, but your team may not be doing enough to execute the strategy or they may be doing the wrong things to execute the strategy. It could be a question of not having enough resources to execute or applying the wrong resources.

- **Strategy choice** — Examine the strategy itself. Is the strategy valid in the current market? Have conditions changed since the strategy was developed and adopted? Are the assumptions that underlie the strategy correct and still valid? As opposed to failing to properly execute a strategy, sometimes the strategy itself is the problem. In this case, you should determine if you are going about achieving your goals in the wrong way. Review your strategy to determine if it is still valid in your current environment to achieve your goals.

Element 2: Create Your Sales Organization

> *"A strategy, even a great one, doesn't implement itself."*
>
> *— Jeroen De Flander, Author*

You need an appropriate sales organization to execute your sales strategy. In my experience, I've seen many sales organizations evolve over time to address their company's needs. Sometimes this evolution creates a team that works effectively both in the market and within the company. Often, however, evolutionary change creates dysfunction. Different sales reps with different responsibilities within the sales organization (such as product sales, business development or key accounts) may compete against each other or have conflicting goals. Or they may simply not support each other as they pursue their own agendas.

How well does your sales organization work together? How effective are the different groups in reaching your company's strategic goals?

From one company to another, very few sales organizations are alike. Rather than allowing your sales organization to evolve by reacting only to short-term market conditions or specific customer demands, I recommend designing and installing a sales organization that supports your company strategy and leads you to achieve your long-term, strategic goals.

The next four chapters address the design of your sales organization (Chapter 4: Designing Your Sales Organization) and the various parts used to design your sales organization (Chapter 5: Inside Sales and Field Sales, Chapter 6: Customer Service and Sales Enablement, and Chapter 7: Marketing and Sales Operations).

Element 2: Create Your Sales Organization

Turbine Power Systems*

Turbine Power Systems (TPS) provides maintenance and repair services for small to midsize power generation turbines. The work TPS performs is highly technical and specialized. The industry is fragmented and competitive. Its customers are geographically dispersed. Often, they are power plants servicing mills and refineries or small utilities in rural areas.

When TPS decided to rebuild its sales organization to expand into new markets, it took all these factors into account. TPS tasked their low-tech inside sales team with finding opportunities by developing phone-based relationships with decision makers and influencers at every power plant in their target market. The inside sales team was also trained to spot market trends quickly and direct resources where needed.

TPS used its very technical field sales team to complement the work of the inside sales team. Its field sales reps are typically engineers with extensive power systems experience and expertise. Their job is to close the deals by demonstrating TPS's capabilities and credibility.

Finally, these two sales teams are supported by customer-focused service and marketing professionals. Their job is to ensure customers receive the attention and support necessary to maintain strong relationships between scheduled maintenance events.

By creating a sales organization to support their strategy, TPS grew their revenue and expanded their business to the entire United States, the Caribbean nations and South America.

*Company and individual names have been changed.

Chapter 4: Designing Your Sales Organization

"No one can whistle a symphony.
It takes a whole orchestra to play it."

– H.E. Luccock, Yale Divinity School

How you design your sales organization depends on your strategy – what you're selling, where your target market is, who you're selling to and how you plan to reach your market. These elements of your strategy help you determine where to put your sales resources. Depending on your strategy, you may need an inside sales organization that focuses on lead generation and lead nurturing. You may choose to put a direct field organization in place. You may go to market through agents, distributors or retailers. Or, you may decide to use a combination of these customer-facing sales teams.

In addition to the customer-facing sales teams, your sales organization must also provide support for those teams. Your sales strategy – how you reach your prospects and customers – will guide you in determining the sales enablement support you need to put in place. Your sales team will need tools such as proposal and contract templates, call plans and scripts, and sales collateral covering product brochures, spec sheets and manuals. You will also need to consider online and social media strategies.

Let's take look at the different parts of a typical sales organization. You may implement all parts. But, often as a company is growing and resources are scarce, you may need to choose to implement only a few key components at a time. I recommend designing for the growth of your sales organization so that as you add components you do so in a way that best supports your company's long-term strategy.

In this element, we'll review these parts of the sales organization:

- Customer-facing sales roles
  - Inside sales
  - Field sales – Direct and channel (indirect)
  - Customer service
  - Field service (maintenance services)
- Back-office support roles
  - Sales enablement
  - Marketing
  - Sales operations

Inside sales and field sales are traditional customer-facing sales roles. Their purpose is to sell solutions to customers. Customer service and field service are also customer-facing functions. They address customer and product issues and problems, but they can also play a key role in cross-selling and improving customer satisfaction. Sales enablement, marketing and sales operations are not customer-facing roles, but they provide the back-office support the sales team needs to be effective. In smaller, growing companies, these roles may be handled by a single person or a group of people.

The figure on the following page shows how the various parts of a larger, complex sales organization may fit together.

Customers — Prospects — Customers — Prospects — Customers — Prospects — Customers — Prospects — Customers — Prospects — Customers — Prospects — Customers

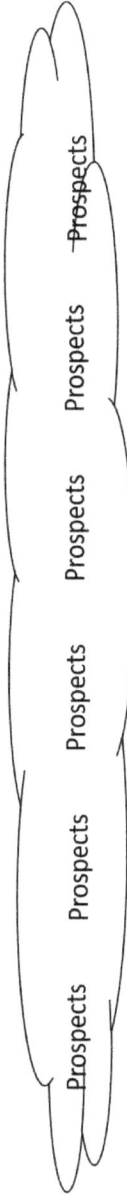

Key Accounts	Geographic Territory / SMB	National Accounts	Industry Accounts	Product Sales	Inside Sales	Customer Service	Field Service

Field Sales

Call Center

| Commission Budgets Forecasting Quotas | CRM Phones Systems | Incentive Plans Recruiting Hiring/Firing Performance Plans | Daily support Messages Travel logistics | Competitive | Sales Collateral / Sales Tools | Demand Gen / Lead Mgmt | Events / Programs | Product Management |

Brand Management

| Finance | Information Technology | Human Resources | Admin | Marketing |

Sales Operations

Sales Enablement

Sales Management

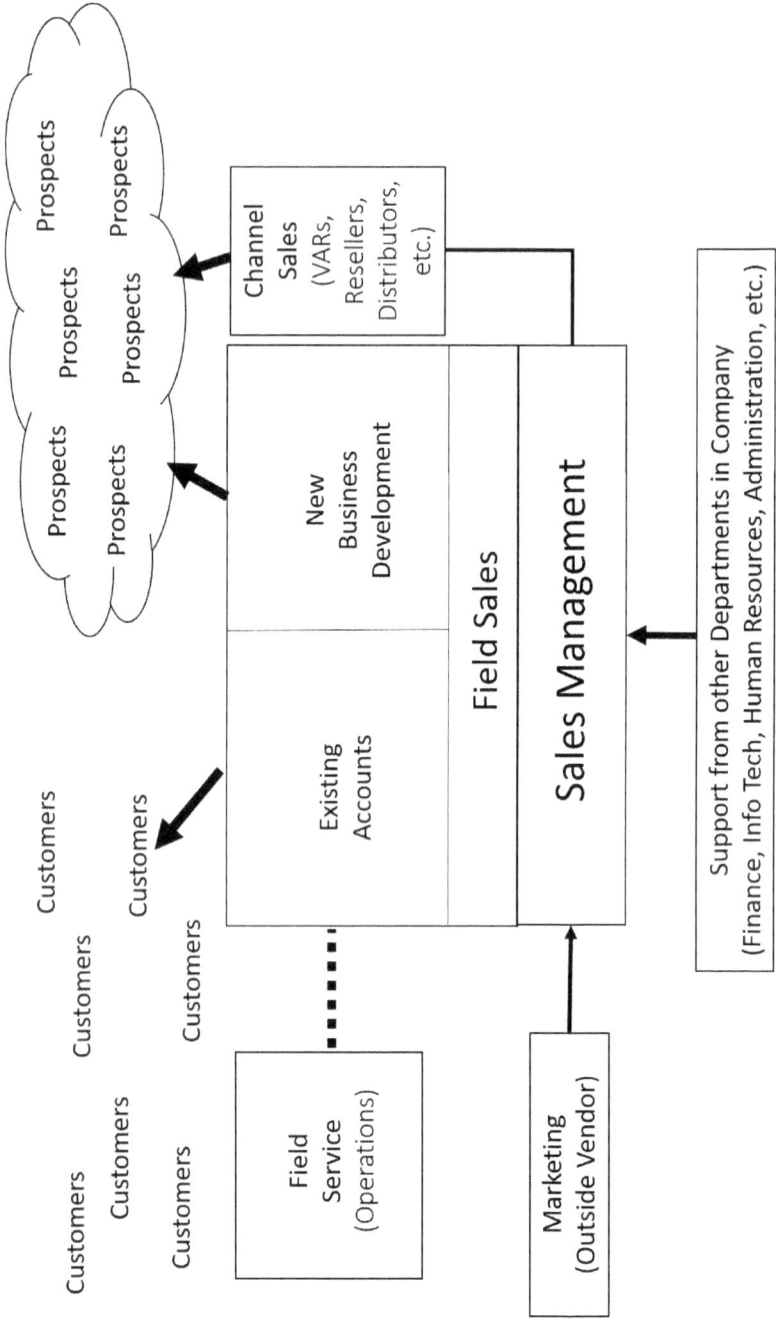

Not all companies need every role. And, certainly not all companies need each role to be filled by one or more individuals. I've worked with many smaller businesses where the sales operations functions were handled by shared services across the company. For instance, the sales organization does not necessarily need dedicated information technology (IT) support. Often, IT is shared across the company. Similarly, the sales team does not necessarily need a dedicated financial analyst. The finance department can provide this support. The same goes for marketing. With respect to field sales, some companies manage well with only territory reps or geographic and national account reps. Other companies outsource some or all their field sales efforts to resellers, distributors or manufacturers' reps.

The second figure (opposite page) shows how a smaller business might design its sales organization with just a field sales team. Some may or may not include a dedicated customer service function. Other small businesses might opt for an inside sales team in place of the field sales team. Still others might employ both. Every business needs to put a team in place that best supports its sales strategy.

The key is to assess your company's needs and design a sales organization that works for your company's strategy, markets and budget.

Chapter 5: Inside Sales and Field Sales

The most visible and impactful positions in your sales organization are your customer-facing sales reps. These reps may be out in the field calling on customers at customer locations (field sales reps) or in your office calling on customers using telephones, social media, video conferences or other remote technologies. As you design your sales organization or make changes an existing organization, you need to determine whether to deploy inside sales, field sales or some combination of both. This chapter covers the benefits of, best environments for and drawbacks of each.

Inside Sales

"One phone call is all it takes!"

The challenge is knowing which phone call will be the one — the one that finds the lead or the one that closes the sale.

Inside sales is basically telesales or telemarketing. But, for many of us, telephone selling has an image problem. Whenever we think about telephone sales, we conjure an image of a sales boiler room with rows of overworked salespeople wearing headsets, dialing for dollars. They are connecting to one call after another, selling timeshare real estate deals or insurance products that we don't need and don't want. In this vision, telemarketers call during dinner or when people are putting their children to bed.

Inside sales has come a long way since the 1970s and 1980s when the negative stereotype got its start. Today's inside sales organizations are very professional. Inside sales representatives are well-trained, highly skilled salespeople. Most often, they are calling on other businesses during normal business hours. To take away the sting of the stereotype, some companies call their inside sales team the "Outbound Call Center."

Benefits of Inside Sales

Consider instituting an inside sales team if you want these benefits:

- **Lower base cost** – Inside sales is often lower in base cost than field sales for two reasons. First, inside sales representatives generally command a lower salary than field sales representatives, although their total compensation can be comparable or higher in some situations. Inside sales representatives also incur fewer expenses than their field counterparts because they have no travel expenses such as airfare, mileage, hotels and meals.

- **Better day-to-day management control** – Your inside sales department is often located in a call center with an on-site inside sales manager. You can log and monitor all your sales representatives' activities and interactions using call center software on voice over IP (VoIP) phone systems. In addition, your inside sales manager can track transaction progress and the state of your sales pipeline in near real time as your sales reps enter information in your CRM system. The close proximity of the inside sales team and tools such as the CRM system enables your inside sales manager to manage the team immediately and effectively.

- **Greater reach** – Since they don't travel, your inside sales team can contact customers anywhere they are – in any geography, any time zone, any industry. Inside sales representatives can also reach many more customers and prospects in a day than most field sales representatives can reach in a week.

Best Environments for Inside Sales

Inside sales teams have proven to be effective for companies operating in these kinds of environments or sales situations:

- **Low-cost, low-margin or low-value products** – In this situation, inside sales is more cost-effective. It only makes sense to incur the higher cost associated with using field sales to sell these types of products when the volume is very high or if the product is sold as an "add on" to the sale of a more complicated solution.

- **Commodity products** – When selling commodity products, the differentiator that closes the sale is usually price or availability. Commodity products have comparable quality. Inside sales is effective and efficient in finding and closing opportunities for commodity products. In-person relationships established by the field sales representative are less of a factor in closing these orders.

- **Large geographic markets** – In geographically dispersed markets, it can be time-consuming and expensive to visit customers. Inside sales provides an effective way to maintain contact with existing customers and qualify prospects and new opportunities.

- **High-volume, high-turnover products** – In markets where customers regularly order a large quantity of products but keep little of their own inventory on hand, inside sales provides an excellent vehicle for staying close to the customer and fulfilling their orders quickly and accurately.

- **High-volume qualification of initial leads** – Not all leads are created equally. For companies that process a high volume of initial leads, it's too expensive to use field sales representatives to qualify initial leads. Inside sales representatives can qualify leads much more quickly, less expensively and at least as accurately.

- **Strict, limited sales process** – In situations where you have a very well-defined, strict sales process, inside sales teams are effective. Since the inside sales team can be more easily managed, they are more likely to follow your strict sales process. Field sales teams, on the other hand, tend to be more independent and more likely to deviate from the sales process if they feel that would be more effective.

Inbound Inside Sales Versus Outbound Inside Sales

Inbound inside sales teams field calls from outside your organization. They react to what the market presents rather than proactively initiating calls. Inbound inside sales teams typically handle these functions:

- **Customer service** – Although customer service is often not associated with "sales," these customer interactions provide opportunities for your customer service reps to sell. Key customer service functions that inside sales reps can handle include managing customer problems, providing information on products and services and escalating customer concerns and issues.

- **Order handling and processing** – As customers call in to place orders, inside sales representatives also can cross-sell and upsell, driving incremental revenue.

- **Lead qualification and lead assessment** – An inside sales team can quickly and efficiently qualify inbound sales leads generated by your marketing team. If you provide your inside sales team with a set of qualifying questions, they can determine a lead's size, time frame for buying and if it is "sales ready."

Outbound inside sales teams generate calls from your company to prospects, customers and the market. They identify opportunities and go after them. Outbound inside sales teams typically handle these functions:

- **Business development** – Inside sales teams are great for prospecting and exploring new markets. With good phone lists, an inside sales representative can make up to 200 calls per day and reach 30 to 40 contacts.

- **Lead qualification** – Like their inbound counterparts, outbound inside sales teams are also highly effective at lead qualification. Outbound sales representatives call to follow up on marketing leads that have not yet spoken with your company sales representatives. Your outbound sales team calls out to contact your lead prospects and qualify them based on questions you develop in advance.

- **Lead nurturing** – Lead nurturing is a campaign that marketing and your inside sales team jointly execute. It is designed to maintain and develop opportunities until the buyer is ready to purchase. While marketing can keep the prospective customer on the hook through email, direct mail and other advertising, an outbound inside sales team is very effective at calling the prospect at preset intervals to provide a personal touch and, if necessary, create urgency to act.

- **Appointment setting** – Businesses that have high transaction rates and depend on a lot of cold calling to reach new customers often use inside sales to qualify prospects and set appointments for their field sales team. By leveraging inside sales to call prospects and set appointments, the company can maximize the time its field sales team and closing specialists spend in front of high-value customers and prospects.

- **Commodity sales** – Outbound sales teams are often used to close sales for commodities where the product is at a low price point and purchase decisions are often based on availability. The inside sales team can uncover and track many opportunities. By closely tracking opportunities, inside sales can time their calls to coincide with customer purchase needs and buying time frames.

- **Customer service** – Just as inbound inside sales teams can effectively cross-sell and upsell during customer service calls, outbound sales teams are also very effective selling to customers when they make calls to follow up on customer inquiries or field service calls. Follow-up calls to make sure customers are satisfied with your products and services provide the outbound sales rep with excellent opportunities to present related offerings.

- **Market surveys and awareness** – Outbound sales calls provide your company with the opportunity to measure customer satisfaction and product effectiveness, ask about competitive offerings and gather a myriad of market information that is available – if the reps just ask customers about these things. Outbound inside sales reps can uncover market opportunities for new products and services. These calls also offer reps the chance to learn about customers' perceptions of your company, brand, products and competitors.

Drawbacks of Inside Sales

Inside sales has two potential drawbacks:

- **Limited depth of relationships** – The lack of in-person, face-to-face interaction can limit the depth of relationships that your inside sales representative can make. Done well, field sales representatives can develop close personal and professional relationships with their customers. Inside sales representatives can have a hard time replicating these close relationships, although as seen in the Turbine Power Systems example at the start of this section, it can be done. When closing key sales, deep relationships can sometimes make the difference between winning the sale and losing it.

- **Less effective at handling complex sales** – Without face-to-face interaction, inside sales representatives may be less effective at handling complex sales. Complex sales often require long cycles of interaction as the sales representative and customer get to know and trust each other. During this time, communication is as much about subtle signs and body language as it is about speaking, letters and emails. Without in-person meetings, inside sales representatives may not have the opportunity to see the subtle signs and body language, which puts them at a disadvantage.

Field Sales

"I have always believed that you cannot run a successful enterprise from behind a desk."

– Louis V. Gerstner, Jr., CEO IBM Corporation (1993-2002)

Field sales primarily refers to the sales representatives that interact directly with your customers face-to-face. Field sales can involve two distinct types of sales teams:

- **Direct sales team** – The direct sales team is your company's field sales reps. They work for your company and are usually paid a base salary plus commission. Their job is to represent your company and no other. They sell your products to a territory or an account set that you define.

- **Indirect or "channel" sales team** – Channel sales teams work independently from your company. The company does not pay them a salary. They earn compensation by selling your products and perhaps products from other companies as well.

Benefits of Direct Sales

Direct sales offers significant benefits to your company when it has complexity in any of these three areas:

- **Complex solution** – When a solution is complex, it requires time and expertise to develop and sell. Direct sales teams can provide both the time and the expertise. Field sales representatives are well trained in their company's products. They also know their market, industry and customers very well. Taken together, deep product expertise and market knowledge put the field sales representatives in an excellent position to develop and sell the complex, custom solutions their customers need and demand.

- **Complex customer relationships** – Complex customer relationships can be critical to market success for some companies. This is especially true for companies with large and key accounts. Often, key accounts have multiple opportunity areas with several sales points. A direct sales representative can invest the time and effort a company needs to cultivate complex relationships with all the influencers and decision makers within an account. Also, the direct sales representative provides the company with the continuity and control needed to maintain long-term relationships and the high levels of customer service and satisfaction that key accounts demand.

- **Complex sales processes** – Complex sale processes require close control of the sales team as they navigate both the sales process and the customer's buying process. Multiple factors can add complexity to the sales process, including size of the transaction, risk perceived by the customer when purchasing or implementing the solution, length of the sales cycle, and government or industry regulations. Any combination of these factors can create a delicate sales balance that requires a sales team that will guide the opportunity through to its close. Since they are closely managed by the company, direct sales teams are in an excellent position to manage that balance.

Best Environments for Direct Sales

The best environments for deploying a direct sales force are those where the company has:

- **High-margin, high-value solutions** – In these situations, customers are investing significant resources to acquire or implement your solution. They expect your company to also invest in the sale to ensure everything proceeds smoothly.

- **Complex solutions** – As noted earlier, direct sales teams are very effective in managing complex solutions as they progress from lead qualification through sale, closing and implementation.

- **Key accounts** – Key accounts are customers or prospects that are important to your company's future growth. They may currently buy a lot of your product and contribute strongly to your revenue, have a lot of influence among customers and prospects in your target markets or have great revenue potential. These accounts are important to your company's future; therefore, it makes sense to commit the resources you need to grow these accounts.

- **National accounts** – National accounts are accounts you sell to that have locations dispersed across the country. A national account may be a key account, but not necessarily. National accounts often require a single point of sales contact to coordinate their orders and activities. For this reason, if the account is large enough and important enough to your company, it's best to assign a direct sales representative responsibility for the account. Otherwise, consider selling to and servicing smaller national accounts with your inside sales team or through another field channel.

Drawbacks of Direct Sales

There are two main drawbacks to implementing a direct sales team:

- **Expensive** – Direct sales representatives have higher fixed costs – salaries, benefits, equipment and management – and higher incremental expenses, primarily travel expenses.

- **Cover a limited number of accounts/customers** – Since there are a limited number of hours in a day and a limited number of days in a week, month or year, direct sales representatives are limited in the number of customers they can call on. Therefore, effective sales executives focus their direct sales efforts on key accounts or key territories. All other prospects and accounts must be handled through other channels such as inside sales or channel sales (aka indirect sales).

Channel Sales

"Direct sales teams establish your customer reach. Channel sales partners extend it."

Channel sales are driven by distributors, agents, value-added resellers (VARs) and manufacturers' representatives. Some companies will also include original equipment manufacturers (OEMs) as part of their channel sales force.

Typically, a channel sales team does not sell multiple competitive products if the line they represent is high-margin and highly specialized, like banking equipment, for example. In the banking industry, there are a limited number of manufacturers of cash-handling equipment. As a result, distributors and agents leverage their value by carrying and representing only one cash-handling manufacturer at a time. In rare instances, they may represent more than one manufacturer, but they do not carry competitive product lines.

At the lower end of a market, as the products become more commoditized, distributors and agents will carry multiple competitive product lines, for example, office supplies such as paper, ink and toner.

Benefits of Channel Sales

Channel sales can offer a company these significant benefits:

- **Lower fixed costs** – Channel sales teams present lower fixed costs than a direct sales team. You pay channel sales teams only when they purchase your products for resale or integration into their own solutions. Since the channel sales organization assumes the direct costs of selling, you normally pay a higher commission to the channel sales rep or provide your product to them at a substantial discount (wholesale price). Therefore, your gross margins are lower, but your net margins may be the same since you avoid many of the direct selling costs. Some companies choose to assign a sales manager to manage their channel sales.

- **Greater reach** – Channel sales organizations offer greater reach into markets that your company might not be able to afford otherwise. Often, channel sales organizations have extensive relationships in place within your target market. Many are industry or solution specialists who can better position your offering within your target market. Distributors, agents, VARs and manufacturers' reps have a depth of expertise and a range of customer relationships that would take a new company years to develop.

- **Increased speed to market** – Since channel partners are already established in a market with branding and customers, you can enter the market more quickly than if your company needed to build out the infrastructure, hire the sales representatives and develop customer relationships.

- **Established logistics so you can scale and focus** – The established channel partner has an established customer base and sales team. The channel partner manages the logistics associated with the sales team, lead generation, sales calls and so on. This frees your company to focus on uncovering customer and market needs and developing your products and services to meet those needs.

Best Environments for Channel Sales

Channel sales organizations are best employed by companies and industries having these characteristics:

- **Large, geographically dispersed markets** – In these markets, you need direct customer contact, but you cannot afford to employ the number of direct sales representatives you would need to sell effectively to the market.

- **Moderately complex products or solutions** – These demand hands-on sales specialists, but the volumes or the margins are not high enough to justify incurring the cost of a direct sales rep. Often, companies support channel sales teams with their own product specialists when needed.

- **Small or midsized business** – Your company may not have the resources needed to employ a direct sales team. Channel sales teams are an excellent way to leverage your resources and gain market reach that would otherwise be unaffordable.

- **Well-established and accepted channels** – In certain industries, channel sales organizations and networks are well established and accepted. Examples of these industries include food distribution and building materials.

Drawbacks of Channel Sales

Although the advantages of employing a channel sales team can be compelling, there are drawbacks:

- **Less control** – Since the channel sales organization is an independent company, you have less control over their sales representatives. If your products and services are a significant percentage of the agent's or VAR's revenue, then you may exert a stronger influence over how they sell and to whom they sell. However, if your offering is a relatively minor part of the overall success of the agent's or VAR's business, then you will have little leverage to influence their behavior.

- **Limited customer interaction** – Your channel sales partner owns your customer relationships. Generally, they will not be inclined to share customer contacts. In some cases, you may not know who your end users are unless they work directly with you for product support or service.

- **Less exclusivity** – Channel sales organizations may not agree to represent your products exclusively. They may also sell competitive products and services depending on their customers' needs or the amount of commission or margin they make on a sale. Similarly, channel sales organizations may not have any loyalty, contractual or otherwise, to you and your products. They may drop your line and move to sell competitive lines with little or no notice. If this occurs, that agent's customers may choose to buy your competitors' solutions rather than yours.

- **Less predictable revenue** – Channel sales partners may or may not provide you with accurate sales forecasts. Your channel partners are also unlikely to provide clear visibility to their sales pipeline of customer opportunities. This lack of visibility makes direct forecasting difficult.

- **Lower gross margins** – Channel sales partners often require 30% to 50% discounts off your retail list price. This is your cost of sales and access to the market. The discount offsets costs you would incur if you went to market with a direct sales team, including salaries, commissions, office leases, phones and travel.

Additional Questions/Factors to Consider With Channel Sales

When evaluating whether to work with channel sales partners, there are additional questions and factors to consider:

- **How do you help your channel partners make money?** (i.e., what's in it for them) Your channel sales partners sell your product to make money. Your product may complement other lines they sell. Or, it may add functionality to their products (OEMs). By offering your line, your partners may also be able to provide additional services such as installation, monitoring or maintenance (VARs).

- **How do your channel partners help you make money?** In addition to selling more products or services than your direct sales team can sell, channel partners may deliver both tangible and intangible benefits to your company. They may extend your market reach or provide additional credibility to your company by association with their brand. They may offer services that complement your product and therefore drive demand. They may provide a lower-cost entry into a market you're not currently selling to because of distance. They may provide market knowledge that you've not yet developed.

- **What additional benefits do the channel partners bring to the table?** Channel partners offer your company access to existing customer relationships, an established sales force, market knowledge, logistics and complementary services. Look for channel partners that can add value to your company.

- **How can you gain information about your customers without communicating directly with them?** Channel sales partners often jealously guard their customer information. Their customers are their livelihood and they will not risk a supplier or vendor taking that relationship away from them. As a result, you must do two things. First, develop a trust relationship with your channel partners. Show them that you want to help them develop their customer relationships rather than take them for yourself. Help your channel partner anticipate their customers' needs. Share information that will make them more effective. Second, develop an independent relationship with your end users that does not threaten your channel partner. Consider support agreements where your field service team provides maintenance and technical support. Also, set up product registrations so that you can communicate product updates quickly. Throughout this process, keep your channel partner informed, building the trust needed for a solid relationship.

Chapter 6: Customer Service and Sales Enablement

Next to your direct sales teams, your customer service field service teams are likely the next most influential group dealing with your customers. Sales enablement supports inside sales, direct sales and customer service. Customer service (including field service) and sales enablement are critical components of your sales organization design. These functions address customer and product issues and problems, and provide support to the sales team so they can focus on selling.

Customer Service

"Your most unhappy customer is your greatest source of learning."

– Bill Gates, founder, Microsoft

Like inside sales, customer service centers can handle calls that are either inbound, outbound or both. Some customer service centers also handle walk-in or in-person calls, although these types of centers are generally found in business-to-consumer (B2C) or retail operations.

Customer service representatives (CSRs) are generally an initial point of contact for customers with a problem. Customer problems can range from minor inquiries to serious issues. Your customer service team needs to have the skills, knowledge and tools to handle nearly all of these. Minor customer inquiries often involve questions about current pricing, expected delivery schedules or product specifications. CSRs can usually answer these questions quickly by searching online product manuals or checking the customer's orders. They may escalate inquiries about serious issues to their manager or to product specialists.

Often, managers provide incentives to encourage their CSRs to maximize the number of calls they handle. Their idea is to make the customer service team efficient – answer a call, resolve the problem, move on to the next call. However, this can be a mistake.

Customer questions and customer dissatisfaction can be great sources of market information and excellent sales opportunities. As Bill Gates points out in the quote above, unhappy customers can teach you a lot about your products – their advantages and shortcomings – and your market.

If a customer calls your customer service team to ask about using your product for an unintended application, effective CSRs will not simply say "no." Train your CSRs in how probe to learn more about the new application and how the customer wants to use the product. Encourage them to ask questions to understand the need driving the customer's question. In turn, this may reveal a new use or market for your product. Or, train the CSRs in how to uncover an opportunity to cross-sell another product or set of products to address the customer's need. Without asking questions of the unhappy customer, these opportunities may never be identified.

The internet provides companies with the opportunity to provide self-service customer service. Since many frequent customer questions address a small number of topics, companies often provide online FAQ (frequently asked questions) pages or applications. FAQ pages and related "knowledge databases" enable companies to dramatically reduce the cost of customer service by reducing or eliminating "live" customer service representatives. The online option is very tempting to implement. However, if you go this route, recognize the downside.

By having customers handle their own customer service, you lose the personal interactions with customers. Sometimes you lose a sense of the market and hidden opportunities to cross-sell and upsell. You may also lose sight of unforeseen applications and uses for your products or, worse, not recognize emerging customer or product problems. With extensive tracking of customer search terms and improvements to artificial intelligence agents, you may offset part of the loss, but you need to weigh the advantages and disadvantages. Your customer service team is an excellent window into your market and your customers; be careful not to lose it.

Field Service

"Sales go up or down; service stays forever."

Like customer service, field service (maintenance and repair) is a great way to learn more about how your products are used by customers.

Your field service team can learn both the applications for which your customer uses your products and where they use them.

Field service technicians work in the locations and environments where your products are used. They see how customers use your products. They talk to the people using your products. Your field service technicians help get your customer's equipment and people back to work when something goes wrong. Your customers have a high level of trust in your field service technicians since they nearly always relieve your customer's pain and frustration when they experience downtime.

As a result of their unique relationship with customers and users, your field service techs understand the market for your products very well. They can be an excellent resource to identify new markets and changes in existing markets. They are also an excellent resource for your product development team as they plan new models and improve the quality of your existing products. Finally, your field service team is in a great position to cross-sell and upsell additional solutions to your customer. They are an important part of your overall sales team.

Sales Enablement

> *"If you don't serve the customer, then your job is to serve someone who does."*
>
> *— Anonymous quote often attributed to Phil Kotler, marketing management guru*

Your customer-facing sales team cannot work well without support. Sales enablement teams provide this support by handling and automating tasks that occupy sales and service representatives' time, time they could be spending directly engaging with prospects and customers. Sales enablement employs a variety of tools and systems to provide the sales team with the information they need to sell to their customers. The sales enablement team also implements processes and deploys programs to make the sales team efficient. Let's look at each of these areas to better understand how sales enablement helps the sales team.

Tools

Tools provide customer-facing sales representatives with the information they need to sell effectively. Tools may help shorten the selling process. They may also reinforce the company's brand with the customer. Tools are maintained and updated by the sales enablement team. If your company is not big enough yet to have a dedicated sales enablement team, assign specific people to creating and maintaining the tools your sales reps depend on.

Common tools include:

- **Forecasts** – Sales representatives put together monthly, quarterly and annual forecasts with assistance from sales enablement to provide the reps and management with a view of expected sales by units and revenue. Forecasts are detailed by time frame, product and customer. Most forecasts include a "likely to close" indication, usually expressed as a percentage.

- **Collateral** – Documents that sales representatives send to customers or leave with them to reinforce product information and brand image.

  - **Brochures** – 1- to 2-page sell sheets that describe the company, its products and solutions.

  - **Spec sheets** – Usually one-page product information sheets that provide technical specifications about a product, rather than sales information.

  - **White papers** – Technical or non-technical papers written about a product or market. White papers are usually several pages long and are written as if created by an objective third party, although they are often commissioned by the company delivering the white paper.

  - **Premiums** – Tchotchkes and other small, branded articles or gadgets that sales representatives leave with prospects and customers to remind them of your brand.

> Common premiums are pens, notepads and water bottles. Ideal premiums are both branded and related to the company's products.
>
> o **Branded swag** – Branded premiums are considered "swag." Going beyond premiums, though, swag may also include branded clothing such as hats, shirts, jackets and other apparel.

- **Competitive library** – A repository of competitive information gleaned from internet and field research, collections of competitive marketing materials, publicly available pricing, strategies, and anything else the sales team learns about competitive practices, strategies and tactics. An up-to-date and complete competitive library can be a huge advantage to your sales team when selling in competitive situations.

- **Templates** – Standardized formats for customer communications. Templates reinforce your brand and reduce the work a sales representative does to deliver complete communications with a professional look.

- **Contract forms** – Contracts define the agreement between your company and your customer. Sales enablement maintains files of all customer contracts. They make available the standard contract approved by legal for sales representatives to present to customers at the start of contract negotiations. Customers may negotiate terms in the contract; but by starting with your company's standard terms, you are more likely to have the final agreement include the points that are important to you and your company.

- **Proposal templates** – Sales representatives generate proposals for most, if not all, initial customer transactions. Customers may conduct ongoing transactions (reorders) based on earlier proposals. Sales enablement should maintain proposal templates to ensure the sales team delivers high-quality proposals with a consistent brand, message and offer. Proposal templates also reduce the work associated with creating the proposal since sales reps are not creating a unique proposal from scratch each time.

- **Presentations** – Sales enablement should customize and maintain sales presentations for the sales team. This ensures consistent messaging and branding.

- **Metrics tracking reports** – Every successful sales team is driven by goals. The sales enablement team should track the metrics and report progress toward achievement of the goals. Metrics are shared with both the sales team and management so that everyone can ensure that the business and the sales representatives are on a path to success. For smaller companies, metrics are often developed and maintained by an analyst in the company's financial planning and analysis group.

Systems

Systems are tools and processes which are combined to make it easier to store data and track information. Many systems are computer-based to manage the large amounts of data generated by the selling process.

Some of the systems most used in sales include:

- **CRM** – Customer relationship management (CRM) systems track all the data associated with customers and prospects including the company's contacts with the customers and prospects, opportunities, past transactions, planned contacts and competitive information. CRM systems make it easier for both sales representatives and their managers to track all the opportunities the sales team is working on and ensure they do not overlook or miss necessary steps to ultimately close business.

- **CPQ** – Configure, price, quote systems provide an up-to-date tool and process for sales representatives to deliver accurate price quotations to customers. CPQ systems are especially important when the product or solution is custom, complex and difficult to configure. The CPQ system ensures that solutions are configured properly with all prerequisite and co-requisite features. The CPQ system may also feed a proposal template to generate clear, professional proposals.

- **Cloud or SharePoint servers** – Central server systems enable teams of sales representatives to easily share information and collaborate on opportunities and projects. All documents reside in a central location accessible via the internet or a virtual private network (VPN).

- **Sales practices** – Every company should define its set of commonly accepted sales practices to make sure that sales representatives present themselves and the company professionally and consistently. Sales practices also protect the company's brand in the market. Finally, sales practices reduce the chance that sales reps will commit or expose the company to legal or financial risks the company is not willing to accept.

Processes

Several processes can be used to manage the flow of information through the sales organization. The sales enablement team facilitates these processes, freeing up the sales representatives to focus on selling and customer-facing activities.

Here's a sampling of processes your sales enablement team could handle:

- **Information flows** – Data and information are captured regularly by your sales team. Much of it is valuable to both individual opportunities and to the overall sales and marketing strategy of the company. Inside sales reps and field sales reps can enter the data into the CRM and other systems. But you may need to dedicate support resources either as full-time or part-time positions to define the processes that capture and record the data. Support resources may also be valuable for analyzing data and turning it into actionable information.

- **Expense management** – Field sales representatives can incur substantial expenses while selling. All the expenses must be tracked, recorded and reimbursed in a timely fashion. Certainly, sales representatives can manage their own expense accounts. However, to maximize your sales representatives' time in the field with customers, you may elect to have a sales enablement team manage all the paperwork (even if it's electronic) associated with expense management. By some estimates, reconciling and managing expenses can take a sales representative 1 to 2 hours per week. This is time that would be better spent on selling activities.

- **Commissions and compensation** – Your sales representatives need to be paid for the sales they close. They may also need to reconcile their commissions against draws you've paid them. Many sales representatives will maintain a "shadow" accounting system to reassure themselves that they have been properly paid. All this additional work should not be done by sales representatives. They need to be spending their time with customers and prospects. Sales enablement should ensure that sales representatives are paid correctly and promptly.

- **Business intelligence** – To sell effectively in a market, your sales representatives need as much information about the market as they can manage. They will want to know about target markets, demographics, ideal customer profiles, target customer profiles, key decision-maker names, influencers, and customer likes and dislikes. They will even want to know personal information about who they need to meet and sell to. In addition, sales representatives will want to know about competitors — their products and offerings, who they target, pricing, discounts and a whole host of competitive information. Finding this information takes a sales representative away from selling and other customer-facing activities. Business intelligence is best developed and delivered by your sales enablement team.

- **Analytics** – A sales team amasses volumes of data and information about sales, revenue, costs, unit sales by product, sales by geography and industry, win/loss information and on and on. Your company should use this information to its advantage. Sales enablement should perform the analytics your business needs to determine product and market trends, identify successful and unsuccessful sales programs, evaluate sales rep performance and measure customer value. The number and scope of available analytics is limited only by imagination and business needs. However, do not overwhelm your management system with too many measures. Use and measure only what will drive your business forward; otherwise, you may succumb to "analysis paralysis."

Programs

To support the field and customer-facing sales team, sales enablement manages various sales programs that assist the sales efforts, including:

- **Communications** – Your sales team needs to communicate with your customers and prospects on a regular basis. Sometimes they are communicating multiple times a day; other times it's weekly, biweekly or monthly. Sometimes, less frequently. Sales enablement can assume the burden of communications programs that move customers and prospects forward in the sales process. Communications programs may include email, appointment setting, proposal generation, regular sending of brochures or other collateral, and physical mailings.

- **Incentives** – Sales executives may implement contests and bonuses that reward sales representatives for specific activities or results. Examples of sales contests may be races to land the largest number of new customers, fast-start contests to generate a specified number of sales or amount of revenue by a certain date, or product contests that reward sales reps who sell the most units of a new product during a quarter. Sales enablement manages these programs, tracking sales information for all participants and determining winners.

- **Pilots and trials** – Often in major sales, or sales that change how customers conduct their business, sales representatives will provide the customer with a trial product. Or, they may conduct a pilot installation to verify that the proposed solution will deliver the promised benefits. Sales representatives are integrally involved in pilots and trial programs, especially as the contact point for the customer. However, sales enablement may manage the programs from the company's side. Sales enablement will manage logistics, measure results and ensure that any problems that may negatively affect the customer's experience are corrected promptly.

- **Loaners** – Loaners are like trials. Your company may loan products or software to a customer or prospect for a limited period. The loaned equipment allows the customer to test the product and assess its benefits within their environment. The sales enablement team manages all aspects of the loaner program including inventory assignment, scheduling, logistics to and from the customer location and refurbishment of the equipment upon its return. Sales enablement ensures that every customer has an excellent loaner experience.

- **Social media** – Social media is an important tool for companies to communicate with their customers, prospects and the overall market. The sales enablement team should manage social media communications designed by marketing, both inbound and outbound. Central management of social media ensures a consistent message and support of your sales and marketing strategies.

- **Events** – Events include all internal and external sales functions such as conferences, trade shows, product announcements, sporting events and sales meetings. Events require extensive planning to ensure a positive experience for everyone involved: sales reps, customers and executives.

Element 2: Customer Service and Sales Enablement

Planning includes agenda setting, presentations, venue, audio/visual equipment, hotel, transportation, meals and VIP management. Your sales enablement team should plan and execute events for your sales organization.

Chapter 7: Marketing and Sales Operations

Marketing and sales operations are essential components needed to complete your sales organization design.

Marketing

> *"Don't find customers for your products,*
> *find products for your customers."*
>
> *– Seth Godin, author and marketer*

Your marketing team also supports the customer-facing sales team. While sales enablement focuses on the processes and back-office work associated with keeping the sales representatives in front of customers and prospects, marketing focuses on:

- Creating the messages the company delivers to customers and the market

- Increasing brand awareness in the target market

- Generating and qualifying leads for the sales team

- Tracking competitive activity

- Positioning and managing the products the company offers

In some cases, sales enablement and marketing may have overlapping roles, but marketing's role is quite different from that of sales enablement. Marketers bring a different set of skills and a different perspective. Where sales enablement is tactical, marketing is strategic. Sales enablement provides the resources needed to execute the tasks and processes that sales reps would otherwise do to keep their commitments to customers and close sales. Marketing works to find and qualify the prospects that sales will approach. In addition, marketing develops the tools that sales reps use to advance the customer toward a transaction close.

Areas of responsibility for marketing include:

- **Branding** – Creating the company's brand and image. Promoting and protecting the brand such that it becomes valuable.

- **Messaging** – Developing, honing and maintaining the message the company delivers to the market.

- **Public relations** – Managing press relations and ensuring the company and its products are portrayed positively in the press. Creating positive stories about the brand or company to place in appropriate media. During a crisis and in the event of bad publicity, marketing communications or public relations crafts the company's response and manages the crisis to minimize damage and sales disruptions.

- **Advertising** – Developing advertising and placing advertisements in media to promote the company, brands and products.

- **Lead generation** – Creating interest in the company, brand and products such that prospects identify themselves as interested in learning more or becoming a customer.

- **Lead qualification** – Qualifying leads to determine if they are within the company's target market. Passing qualified leads to sales for action.

- **Collateral** – Designing and creating all collateral. Ensuring consistent branding and messaging. Developing collateral for target audiences and markets. Marketing's role here is different from sales enablement as marketing is the creator of collateral while sales enablement maintains the collateral for use by the sales reps. In smaller companies, these roles will overlap.

- **Proposal templates** – Writing proposal boilerplate language that sales reps can modify for specific opportunities. Creating templates so sales can create customized proposals with consistent branding and messaging. As done with collateral, marketing creates the proposal templates and sales enablement maintains and uses them on behalf of the sales team.

- **Presentations** – Creating product and solution presentations that sales can customize to address sales opportunities at various stages of the sales cycle. Maintaining consistent branding and messaging.

- **Competitive tracking** – Tracking competitors' offerings, messaging and branding. Staying fully aware of competitors' positioning, target markets, key customers and pricing as they stand by themselves and relative to your own products.

- **Product management** – Working with sales and product development to create and maintain a multiyear product roadmap. Anticipating market needs and market changes. Incorporating these into the product plans.

Sales Operations

"Our business is about technology, yes.
But it's also about operations and customer relationships."

– Michael Dell, founder and CEO, Dell

Sales operations provides non-sales enablement support to the sales organization. In a larger company, sales operations may be its own department. In a smaller company, sales operations may consist of functional positions that overlay and support the sales organization. The positions may be either full-time or part-time. These individuals have expertise in finance, human resources, information technology (IT) services, administration and legal:

- **Finance** – Key responsibilities for the finance overlay are setting up and tracking budgets, tracking quota attainment, consolidating and tracking sales forecasts, and managing the commission calculations and payments. With respect to quotas, while finance may track quota attainments, quotas themselves should be assigned by the sales manager.

- **Human resources (HR)** – The HR specialists are responsible for recruiting sales personnel from both within and outside the company. They also provide advice and guidance for creating incentive plans and performance plans. They provide guidance to managers when hiring or firing employees. HR specialists also manage interactions with the company's benefits programs.

- **Information technology (IT)** – IT has responsibility for providing access to data, communications and associated technology. They put the systems in place, protect the data, determine user access permissions and train users on how to use technology, equipment and applications. Technology typically includes applications such as CRM systems, phones, computers, networks, Wi-Fi and virtual private networks (VPNs). IT will also interface and negotiate with service providers and technology vendors. They ensure that data is protected from attacks (malicious, accidental and benign) and is backed up in a safe location for future recovery, if needed.

- **Administration** – Administrative support covers traditional support (typing, data entry, answering phones, calendar management, taking messages, managing mail – email or otherwise) as well as order entry and other necessary mundane tasks that accompany the sales process.

- **Legal** – The legal specialist on the sales operations team has two roles. First, this specialist finds solutions to contractual issues so that a sale can be made while protecting the company from unforeseen or unreasonable liabilities. Second, this specialist protects the company and sales team members from taking actions that violate laws, regulations or the company's ethical standards.

Depending on the size, number or complexity of transactions

your sales team generates, a company may assign dedicated legal resources to the sales team. The legal specialist will provide guidance in contract negotiations, maintain contract files, track legal obligations, provide guidance to the sales team on handling legal and ethical situations, develop standard-term contracts and review proposals to customers that may commit the company to future actions or liabilities.

Element 3: Build Your Plans

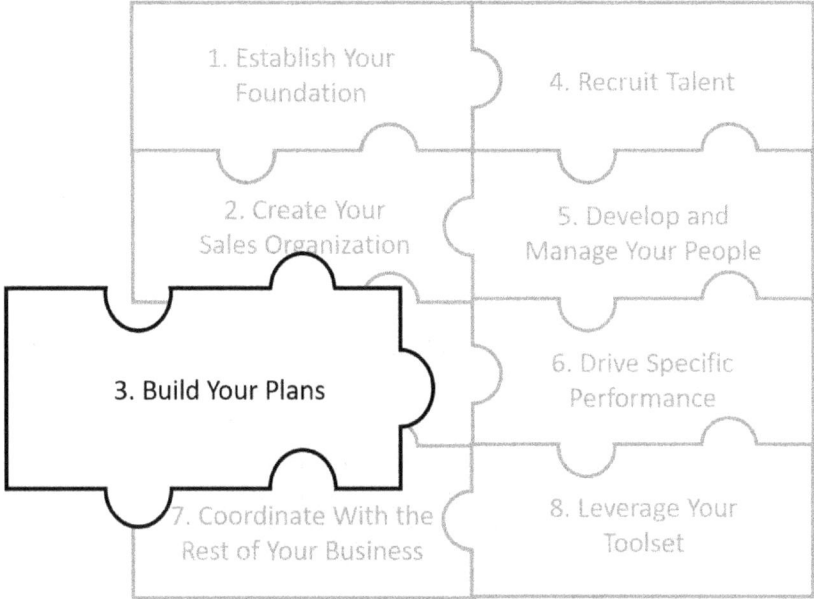

"Plan your work and work your plan."

– Multiple sources

Planning is an ongoing process. Maintaining planning discipline is important. Most companies engage in a thorough planning process annually. There are four key elements to the planning process: data collection, strategic planning, communications and review:

- **Data collection** – This occurs before developing the plan, ideally 6-12 months before. It includes collecting information on the market, competition, product sales and forecasts, and doing a SWOT analysis. SWOT is an analysis of a company's strengths, weaknesses, opportunities and threats. In a traditional SWOT, the strengths and weaknesses relate to the company's internal strengths and weaknesses. Opportunities and threats are generated by external factors such as the market, competition or technology.

- **Strategic planning** – Plans can be strategic, which involves reviewing current and past strategies and plans, defining goals for the current plan and setting new strategies. You are also likely to build associated action plans and communicate those plans to everyone in your organization.

- **Communications** – Plans can be communicated through traditional means such as memos and presentations. Or, your company may opt for a more creative means such as a kick-off meeting to celebrate the start of each new business year.

- **Review** – Following the initial plan development, you should conduct regular reviews, no less frequently than quarterly, and at all levels within the organization. Plan reviews provide your management team with the opportunity to measure progress against the plan, including results versus goals, actions completed and changes in the market. Reviews are an excellent time to update plans or adjust strategies in response to actual market conditions.

The following chapters cover strategic planning (Chapter 8: Strategic Planning), creating and implementing sales territories (Chapter 9: Setting Up Territories) and creating sales plans for those territories (Chapter 10: Creating Territory Plans).

Element 3: Build Your Plans

Data Storage Services*

Data Storage Services (DSS) provides onsite and offsite backup storage systems to small and mid-sized businesses across a range of industries. The systems include both storage appliances that back up local servers and desktop systems as well as cloud storage to provide additional protection and redundancy. DSS provides a full range of storage backup solutions.

Through much of its history, DSS focused its sales team on finding new customers wherever they could. Territories were loosely defined and their strategy was to work hard and make a lot of phone calls.

In the late 2000s, DSS's investors demanded better revenue growth and improved margins. To achieve these goals, DSS put a formal strategy in place for the first time. Their strategy identified target markets and ideal customer profiles. Based on the strategy, DSS redeployed its sales force with defined territories, clear sales goals and strong marketing support.

DSS's revenue growth outpaced their competitors' growth and their margins improved by focusing on more desirable prospects and customers. By having a plan, they accomplished this within three years.

*Company and individual names have been changed.

Chapter 8: Strategic Planning

"Plan for what is difficult while it is easy.
Do what is great while it is small."

— Sun Tzu, ancient Chinese general
and military strategist

As your company's goals change, its strategy must also change over time to account for changing market conditions. Customers grow and shrink. New technologies cause obsolescence of some products and open new markets for others. Sales teams change, bringing new skills and losing existing ones. Competitors enter and leave markets. Customer executives move on to new opportunities. Geopolitical conditions change (e.g., war, peace, treaties, trade pacts, tariffs). Anything and everything could have small and large effects on your strategy.

Make Strategic Planning an Annual Process

Since market conditions constantly change, the most competitive companies develop a clear sales strategy and then update it regularly. This process involves reviewing the strategy statement (see chapter 2), its underlying assumptions and the plan that has been put in place to execute it. At a minimum, your company should update its strategy on an annual basis. Progress reviews and strategy reviews should take place more frequently (i.e., quarterly or monthly).

The first time you create a strategic plan, it may take you and your management team many hours over several weeks. Spending this time is necessary to make sure you understand and document the market factors your company is facing and develop a plan to leverage them so you can achieve your goals. If you are diligent about keeping abreast of your market, subsequent plans will likely take much less time and effort. Quarterly plan reviews should take your management team about 3 to 4 hours to ensure that your company is staying on plan or to adjust the plan midyear. For a complete list of the areas covered in a fully developed strategic plan, see Appendix I — Sections of the Strategic Plan.

When developing your strategic planning process, expect to start about six months before the plan year starts. The following table provides a good list of strategic planning activities and the timing and duration of those activities.

Planning Category	Activity	Timing relative to FYE	Duration
Key Strategy Plan Events	Review current strategy	6 months before	1-2 days
	Define and set goals for new fiscal (plan) year	5 months before	1 week
	Develop strategies and plans to achieve goals	2-4 months before	4-6 weeks
	Adjust plans and goals based on sales forecasts	2	1-2 weeks
	Publish new fiscal (plan) year strategy	0	1 day
Data Collection and Analysis	Conduct SWOT analysis	5 months before	1 day
	Review competition and positioning	5 months before	1-2 days
	Collect forecasts by product, region, key accounts, sales rep, etc.	4-5 months before	1 week
	Consolidate forecasts • Revenue • Product volumes • New accounts • Market penetration	2-4 months before	1 week

Planning Category	Activity	Timing relative to FYE	Duration
	• Market share		
	• Margin		
	• Other		
	Match forecasts to goals	3 months before	1 day
	Review territory assignments, assign sales quotas	3 months – 2 weeks before	2 weeks
	Conduct account/territory planning sessions	0-6 weeks after	1-3 days (each)
Quarterly Reviews	1st Quarter	3 months after	½ day
	2nd Quarter	6 months after	½ day
	3rd Quarter	9 months after	½ day
	Year-end Review	13 months after	½ day
Kick-off Events	Hold new fiscal (plan) year sales kick-off meeting	0-1 months after	1-2 days
	Hold "year-end push" sales kick-off meeting	8-9 months after	1-2 days

Review Current Strategy

The annual strategy planning process should begin six months before the start of your company's new fiscal year. At this point, you are six months into executing your current strategy and it's time for a review. Include your company's key executives (e.g., president, finance leader, sales executive and any other important functional leaders) in your strategy review. Together, you will identify what parts of the strategic plan are working, what parts are not working, how the market has changed and what new opportunities are available to exploit. I strongly suggest conducting your strategy review during a concentrated block of time (usually two to three days) at an off-site location such as the conference room of a local hotel or restaurant.

Based on this review, your key executives define and set goals for the new fiscal year. Setting goals can often take a company from weeks to months to accomplish. When the company is about three months from the start of the new fiscal year, the management team, led by the sales executive, develops the strategy and plans to achieve the company's new sales goals for the next year.

The company's target is to complete its new goals and strategic plan before the start of the new fiscal year.

Conduct a Market Analysis and Collect Sales Forecast Data

Also starting six months before the start of the new fiscal year, your team should collect sales forecast data and do a market analysis. It's important to perform these tasks apart from the strategy review because the data collection and market analysis can take more time and require resources that are not available at an off-site meeting. As you refine your strategy, though, the data you collect and the analyses you perform will contribute to and shape your strategic plan.

Your market analysis should have two parts, a SWOT analysis and a competitive analysis:

- **SWOT analysis** – SWOT stands for Strengths, Weaknesses, Opportunities and Threats. The strengths and weaknesses are internally focused. These are the strengths and weaknesses of your company, your products and solutions, and your team. Opportunities and threats are externally focused. These are the opportunities (positives) and threats (negatives) you face from the market. Opportunities and threats can result from market shifts, new technologies, obsolescence, competitors, changing demographics or pretty much anything you can think of. When conducting a SWOT analysis, it's important to be realistic in your assessment. Also, focus on only the top three to five critical SWOT factors that are likely to have a substantive effect on the business.

- **Competitive analysis** – A competitive analysis is an unbiased review of all your competitors. Include competitors that provide the same or similar product, but from a different source. Also include competitors that provide new or different solutions to your customers' problems. Providers of new or different solutions may indicate disruptive market shifts that could render your offering obsolete. Assess each competitor based on three factors:

  o **Offerings** – Assess each of your competitors' offerings against your customers' needs and against your own offerings. What advantages do they have over your products? Do they cost less? Are they faster or stronger? Do they have better engineering? In what ways are your competitors' offerings less desirable than your own? Are delivery lead times longer? Do your competitors have difficulty delivering the volumes your customers need?

  o **Market position** – Assess each competitor's market position relative to your own. Does the competitor have more or less market share or influence than you have? Are they financially stronger or weaker than your company? Is there a difference in brand strength? Does your competitor have more or less presence and influence in your targeted industries?

o **Strengths and weaknesses** – Map your competitors' strengths and weaknesses against your own strengths and weaknesses (identified in your SWOT analysis). Identify areas where you are strongest and possible gaps in the market you may be able to fill. Also, identify areas that you may need to strengthen to compete more effectively.

Next, collect and consolidate the sales forecasts from your sales team to identify the opportunities for the coming year. Sales forecasts are identified sales opportunities that your sales team can realistically close. Assemble your forecasts by product or solution, region, key account and sales representative. You may also decide to sort forecasted sales by industry or another metric that is important to your business.

Sales forecasts must include all the relevant information associated with each sales opportunity. A sales opportunity is a lead your team has qualified as being real and one for which you have a reasonable likelihood to compete and win. The relevant information associated with each sales opportunity should include:

- Estimated revenue

- Timing to close (date, month or quarter)

- Volume (units expected to be sold)

- Customer names

- Sales representatives' names

- Key opportunities

- Opportunity drivers (what is driving the customer's needs for the products)

- Obstacles to successfully closing the sales

Adjust Plans and Goals Based on the Market Analysis and Forecast Data Collected

At this point, your goals have been set, your strategic statement has been developed, you've analyzed your market and you've collected your sales forecasts. Now, your management team must reconcile the (often lofty) goals and current strategic plan with your company's reality as shown by the data.

First, confirm that the forecasts are reasonable and accurate. This is best done by meeting with your sales team. Discuss the basis for their forecasts. Apply "sanity test" questions to the data. Does the forecasted growth appear too low or too high? How do the volumes compare with prior year volumes? What has changed in the assumptions to account for increases or decreases? Generally, executives and managers who are closest to the field, supported by sales analysis, are in the best position to assess if forecasts are reasonable and accurate.

When you are satisfied that the collected data is good, match your sales goals with the sales forecasts. Are they in line? Do you need to increase or decrease the revenue or volume goals you set? How about the goal for new customers? Is that reasonable? Adjust goals up or down to ensure they are reasonable.

If your goals are significantly higher than the forecasted data, you will need to adjust your strategy to include specific plans to attain those higher goals. Have you included plans for a new product introduction to drive more revenue? Does your strategy call for penetration into new industries, geographies or markets? Have you accounted for the resources you will need to accomplish the drive into new markets? Other strategies might include acquisition of competitors or other companies to grow revenue, acquisition of new customers or penetration of new markets. At this point, you are reconciling your goals and plans with the realities of the market. If your goals are beyond the reach of the forecast, that does not mean they are unrealistic. It does mean, however, that your strategic plan will need to address exactly how you plan to make up the difference.

Review Territory Assignments and Assign Quotas

At this point, you are now about three months before the start of the new fiscal year. It's time to review territory assignments and assign quotas to your sales representatives. Territory assignments are usually kept the same as the prior year with minor adjustments to balance workloads and opportunity across territories. Consistency is important to maintain continuity with existing customers and prospects. Continuity helps to ensure that relationships are maintained, opportunities are developed and commitments are kept.

If you need to create territories, aim for creating a workload that can be reasonably maintained by the sales representative. If a rep has a workload or territory that is too big, the sales representative will most likely:

- Thrash from one opportunity to another while closing only a small number of opportunities.

- Focus only on a few larger or easy-to-close opportunities while allowing the others to be lost to competitors.

- Become burned out by trying to do a stellar job on all opportunities to the detriment of his or her own personal well-being.

Next, assign quotas with a realistic opportunity to meet or exceed the quota. Unrealistic quotas demoralize and demotivate sales representatives, as they see no path to success. This does not mean, though, that every sales representative should or will achieve 100% quota attainment. Nor does it mean that quotas should equal forecasted sales revenue or volume.

Sales quotas should be a combination of three inputs: the sales goal for the company (apportioned to the individual sales territory), the forecasted sales and some "stretch" sales goals. Stretch sales goals are the difference between the sales quota and sales forecast. They represent sales due to a combination of unknown "stretch factors" that invariably contribute to business opportunities in the coming year.

Stretch factors include opportunities arising from market or business changes that favorably affect one or more customers in a territory. One of these changes could be an unexpected customer order. Or your customer could receive an unexpected order that drives a much larger volume of demand for your products. Other changes can result from natural disasters such as a construction boom following a hurricane, flood or tornado. Stretch factors also include new product announcements that drive new orders. Usually, forecasts reflect only current products sold to existing customers. So, you need to increase the forecasts to account for new products that will be available for the sales team to sell. Finally, stretch factors also account for increased sales representative productivity when they are motivated to perform at a higher level. Sales representatives are competitive by nature. When they are challenged with a goal, particularly one that is realistically attainable, they will often succeed in making or surpassing the goal.

Publish Your New Fiscal Year Strategy

Shortly before the start of the new fiscal year, commit to next year's goals and strategy and share them with your sales team. They must know your commitment to the goals and strategy, so they will be prepared to execute on Day 1. Without a clear understanding of your goals and strategy, and a clear understanding of how each sales representative contributes to the goals and strategy, most sales reps will pursue a direction that either is easiest to execute or is most beneficial to themselves. These paths may or may not coincide with the company's goals and strategy.

To achieve this alignment, I recommend holding a formal kick-off event at the start of the new fiscal year. The kick-off event is often a half-day meeting designed to present the company's plan for the new year and get the sales team pumped up to drive success. The management team presents the company's goals for the coming year and its strategy to accomplish them. The kick-off meeting also provides an opportunity to announce territory changes, quota assignments and changes to the commission plan. This kind of transparency about goals and your expectations for the sales team and individual sales representatives is important to ensure your entire team is executing against the same strategy and is fired up to succeed.

Around the time of the kick-off event, individual sales teams should conduct territory planning sessions to identify current opportunities and develop their plans to attain their assigned sales goals. Individual sales representatives should also do this. Finally, over the course of the year, the sales executive should conduct regular (at least quarterly) reviews of the territory sales plans, focusing on execution and year-to-date attainment. Regular reviews give the sales teams and management the opportunity to update their plans to reflect market changes and plan effectiveness.

Chapter 9: Setting Up Territories

"My success, part of it certainly, is that I have focused in on a few things."

– Bill Gates, founder, Microsoft

In Chapter 8: Strategic Planning, we discussed the importance of assigning territories and setting quotas for the sales reps selling in those territories. Why is it important to set up territories? How do you go about setting up territories?

Sales territories define the customers and prospects your sales representatives are assigned to call on. Sales representatives often request larger territories assuming that greater territory size presents them with more opportunities to sell. Their logic is that in a larger territory there are more companies, hence more sales opportunities. However, I have found that sales representatives become less productive with large territories. Sales representatives who focus their sales efforts on a well-defined smaller territory usually find and close more sales and larger sales.

You can set up sales territories in a variety of ways. A common way is by geography. For instance, a sales representative might be assigned a set of zip codes, an entire state or multiple states. Geographic territories are effective when you have low market penetration and are aiming to cover customers and prospects that are evenly dispersed across multiple geographies, such as the United States.

However, you may want to consider other criteria for defining territories, such as customer size, industry, markets the customers serve, or new accounts versus existing accounts. Let's look at some of the common methods of defining sales territories, when they would be used and what the sales rep focuses on in that territory.

Geographic Territories

Setting up sales territories by geography is the most easily understood and straightforward way to define the sales representative's scope of responsibility. Typically, the geographic territory is defined by physical or civic boundaries. In a business that sells to customers throughout the United States, sales territories may be defined by states or by region – Northeast, Midwest, West, South. If a company has multiple sales representatives in an area like New York City, for example, the territories might be smaller and more specifically defined (e.g., commercial buildings between 42nd Street and 59th Street, west of 5th Avenue).

Geographic territories are easy to define and easy to understand. However, one geographic territory may have a vastly different number of opportunities than another territory. In the New York City example, a 100-square block territory on the West Side of Manhattan may have 2 to 3 times as many opportunities as another 100-square block territory on the Lower East Side of Manhattan or in Queens. Another drawback of geographic territories deals with size and distances. Two geographic territories in the same state may offer a similar number of opportunities. However, one sales representative might be traveling long distances by car or plane and spending 2 to 4 days each week away from home to call on customers. The other sales representative might be within a 1- to 2-hour drive from customers and rarely needs to travel away from home.

Geographic territories are commonly used by new businesses that have no established customer relationships, are not industry-specific in their product appeal and have non-complex products.

Industry-Defined Territories

Industry-defined sales territories are appropriate when a company's products or solutions have specific industry applications. For example, an application development business may create software applications for a specific industry's needs such as financial services, video production or traffic monitoring. In manufacturing, a company may sell its products or services to specific industries such as automotive, industrial pipes or aviation.

In industry-defined sales territories, industry knowledge is critical. Industry knowledge may be application-specific, where detailed specifications, processes or information flows are most important. Or, industry knowledge may be more general such as market information, competitive knowledge or industry relationships. In all cases, reps in companies that set industry-defined territories need to know their industries as well as or better than they know their own products and solutions.

Product or Specialty Territories

Product or specialty territories are ones where the product or service is most important. In a product-specific territory, the product or solution the company offers is valued, specialized and uncommon. The product usually commands a premium price because of its value and scarcity. Product specialists typically sell products that are on the leading or cutting edge of technology. Or, the products are protected by intellectual property patents that competitors cannot penetrate.

Companies with complex products, such as medical devices, often employ product specialists. Here, they may have one set of sales reps focused on medical imaging devices like CT scanners or magnetic resonance imagers (MRI) and other sales reps focused on different devices such as catheters or implants.

New Business Development Territories

As the name implies, reps with new business development territories focus on developing new business or closing new customers. These territories require a "hunter" sales representative, someone who is willing and able to find new opportunities with customers the company has not yet done business with. Reps in these territories do a lot a lot of prospecting, cold calling and lead development, and they often deal with rejection.

Reps in new business development territories are working on many opportunities at any given time. These reps need to communicate well with customers and view rejection (i.e., customers saying "no") as part of the sales process. These reps do not take rejection personally and often view "no" as meaning "not yet." They need to be strong optimists who believe that the next deal can be found in the next sales call.

Reps in new business development territories often work in parallel with reps in sales territories that have established customers. But the mindset and responsibilities of the new business development sales representative are quite different from those of the sales representative working with established accounts.

Key Account Territories

Reps in key account territories focus on important customers who demand or require focused attention because of their importance to your company. Key accounts may be high-value customers because of their sales volume. Or, they may be influential players in the company's target market. In either case, you want to assign key account territories to sales representative who focus on building relationships, customer service, cross-selling and opportunity development. In larger sales organizations and companies, a key account rep may also be an industry specialist or product specialist with in-depth expertise related to the key accounts' industries or products.

National Account Territories

Reps in national account territories function like key account reps. They have the same characteristics, but national account reps usually manage only one or two accounts that are national in size. National account reps often work with local sales representatives who service individual locations or business units, but the national account rep has overall responsibility for the account and the strategy for selling to the account. The national account rep is the customer's primary point of contact.

Chapter 10: Creating Territory Plans

"People do what you inspect, not what you expect."

– Louis V. Gerstner, Jr., CEO, IBM Corporation (1993-2002)

After you have developed a sales strategy for the company, reviewed territories and assigned quotas to your reps, the next step involves developing a plan for each territory.

It's not enough to simply assign targets and quotas to individual accounts or territories. Nor is it enough to set only product targets within territories. These must be done as part of the planning process, but they are not enough.

Complete territory and account plans identify specific opportunities that will drive achievement of the company's sales targets and quotas. In addition, they also identify the activities the sales reps must undertake to achieve their goals, when the activities must be done and who will be responsible for completing the activities. Finally, plans must include milestones and metrics to measure the sales team's progress on the path to success.

Identify the Sales Opportunities, Actions and Accountability Metrics

I recommend communicating the sales strategy to your team and then allowing the sales reps on the front lines to develop specific territory plans. Ask each rep to identify and document all the sales opportunities they foresee in their territories. For each opportunity, they should provide all the details associated with the opportunity, including:

- Name of customer

- Opportunity description

- Projected gross revenue

- Products and services in the opportunity

- Timing – When the opportunity is targeted to close

- Likelihood to close (expressed in a percentage)

Ideally, in an established territory in which the sales rep has been selling for a couple of years or longer, the projected gross revenue of opportunities in established accounts should account for about 80% of the rep's assigned quota. Other account opportunities should present another 50% of the quota. Some of these opportunities will fail to materialize and others will be lost to competitors; but a solid sales rep should close a good number of the opportunities.

The next step is to determine the actions and activities the sales rep (or sales team) must undertake to close each opportunity. Actions may include sales calls on key decision makers or influencers, product demonstrations, proposals and financial models, for example. In addition to identifying the actions, the sales rep should also assign a time frame in which to complete the action and assign a specific person to own responsibility for completing the action. The owners of each action are typically the sales reps themselves, but the owner may be another team member such as a product specialist, sales manager or engineer. In any event, the person assigned must agree to assume ownership.

Finally, identify milestones on the path to success and metrics to measure progress so that the sales rep and manager can assess if they are on track.

The Sales Planning Process chart on the next page summarizes the territory planning process. The overall company sales plan is supported by individual territory plans. The territory plans, in turn, are supported by the plans the sales reps have developed for their customers. Customer plans are made up of how and what products and services the sales rep will sell to those customers. Products and services are further defined by number of units to sell (volume) and associated revenue. When planning for revenue and volume, it is helpful to separate them by "flow," "likely" and "reach." Flow opportunities are those that the rep is 100% certain will occur, given that the rep and company do their jobs and are responsive to the customer.

Element 3: Creating Territory Plans

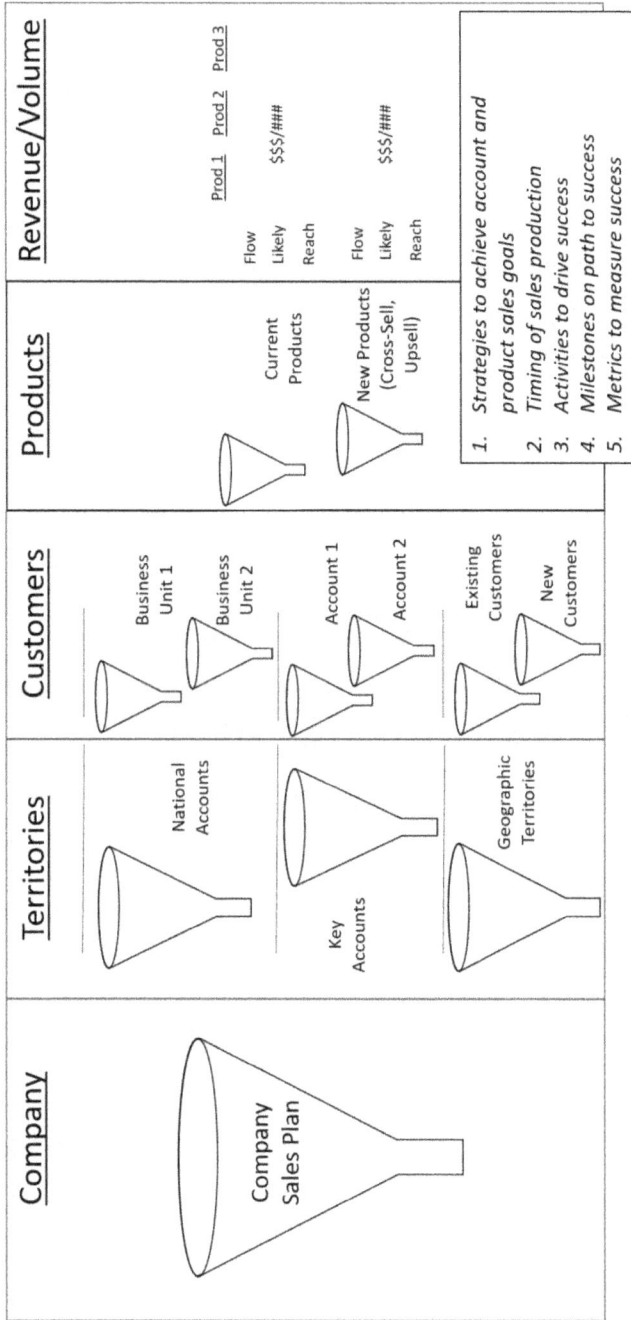

Sales Planning Process

Company — Company Sales Plan

Territories — National Accounts, Key Accounts, Geographic Territories

Customers — Business Unit 1, Business Unit 2, Account 1, Account 2, Existing Customers, New Customers

Products — Current Products, New Products (Cross-Sell, Upsell)

Revenue/Volume — Prod 1, Prod 2, Prod 3; Flow, Likely, Reach $$$/###; Flow, Likely, Reach $$$/###

1. Strategies to achieve account and product sales goals
2. Timing of sales production
3. Activities to drive success
4. Milestones on path to success
5. Metrics to measure success

Likely opportunities are those that have a better than 50% likelihood of closing and being awarded to the company. The sales rep will need to fulfill various responsibilities such as sales calls, demonstrations, etc. to win the opportunity, but the rep has high confidence that your company will prevail. Reach opportunities are those where the rep has less than 50% confidence that he or she will win the opportunity. In addition to performing the right activities, other undefined decisions must happen to win the opportunity.

When planning for revenue and volume in the chart above, it is helpful to separate the opportunities into "flow," "likely" and "reach" categories. Flow opportunities are those that the rep is 100% certain will occur, given that the rep and company do their jobs and are responsive to the customer. Likely opportunities are those that have a better than 50% likelihood of closing and being awarded to the company. The sales rep will need to fulfill various responsibilities such as sales calls, demonstrations, etc. to win the opportunity, but the rep has high confidence that your company will prevail. Reach opportunities are those where the rep has less than 50% confidence that he or she will win the opportunity. In addition to performing the right activities, other undefined decisions must happen to win the opportunity.

Finally, the Sales Planning Process chart list five additional steps that the sales rep must take to develop a complete plan.

1. Develop strategies to achieve the account and product sales goals. These strategies should be clearly documented by the rep.

2. Lay out the expected timing of the sales production. When does the rep expect or plan to close various opportunities? This provides a preliminary sales forecast so that your operations team can develop their build plans to meet demand.

3. Define the activities necessary to drive success. Activities include all the steps the sales rep needs to take to move the customer through the sales process. This step should also

indicate when the rep needs to perform the activities to meet the expected timing of the sales.

4. Identify milestones on the path to success. Milestones enable the sales rep and management to determine if they are making progress and are on schedule to meet their commitments.

5. Set metrics to measure success. Metrics measure the rate of activity necessary to achieve success. Metrics may include number of sales calls made each week or number of product demonstrations or proposals delivered each month. Metrics should measure activities that are closely tied to success rather than the amount of busy work performed.

Review Plans, Activities and Results

Over the course of the year or sales cycle, effective managers review each sales representative's territory plan on a regular basis directly with the sales representative. Reviews cover more than milestones and key performance indicators, although those are important to include. Reviews also examine the assumptions that underlie the plan. They look at changes in market conditions — competitive threats, advancements in technology and strategy effectiveness — to name just a few areas. Two to four times per year is a reasonable frequency for territory plan reviews. Some sales executives may elect to review their team's plans more frequently if the sales cycle is short or the responsible sales representatives are not on target to achieve quota or goals.

So, how should a manager conduct a territory plan review?

First, look at the territory's performance at a high level. Next, drill down into the performance and the plan by asking probing questions. See Appendix II – Probing Questions for a Territory Review for examples of questions you might ask during a territory review.

These are the goals of regular territory reviews:

- Assess where the sales rep and the company stand relative to performance against the territory plan

- Learn more about the customers, markets and products/services in the territory

- Adjust the territory plan assumptions to reflect current conditions

- Adjust the rep's activities, targets (customers, markets, expectations) and product/service offerings to improve performance and drive revenue faster

The purpose of the territory review is to identify what's driving success, or lack of success, in the territory. It is not a performance review for the sales representative. If the territory review shows that poor results are due to the rep's poor performance, then the manager needs to conduct a separate sales rep performance review. This is covered later in Element 5: Develop and Manage Your People, Chapter 15: Performance Management.

Use Metrics to Monitor Progress

"What gets measured, gets improved."

– Peter Drucker, management guru,
consultant, educator, author

Reviewing territory plans on a quarterly or semi-annual basis is not enough to drive success. A good manager puts metrics in place so the manager can see immediately when performance or results are slipping. As stated in Element 1: Build Your Foundation, goals and metrics are not the same thing. Goals indicate a desired result. Metrics measure progress toward that result. Metrics can also measure the activities necessary to drive results, such as the number of initial calls a sales rep completes each week or the number of presentations a rep delivers each day.

Metrics must be measurable and easily understood by both the sales reps and the manager. Equally important, metrics must be readily available. Ideally, performance metrics should be available to the rep and manager in real time. Some companies update their data in real time or daily; others may provide updates weekly or less frequently. Keep in mind that the less frequent your updates, the less useful your metrics become. The sooner feedback is provided relative to performance events, the more reliably the sales reps will relate the results to their actions and stay on the path to success.

Powerful dashboard tools that present your metrics in a computer or mobile application are available through applications such as PowerBI from Microsoft, Tableau or QlikView. These tools enable you to access your metrics whenever and wherever you need them, whether in the office or while traveling. In the hands of a capable data analyst or even a motivated manager with a penchant for technology, these tools can be quickly implemented to present your data in an effective and compelling format.

Element 4: Recruit Talent

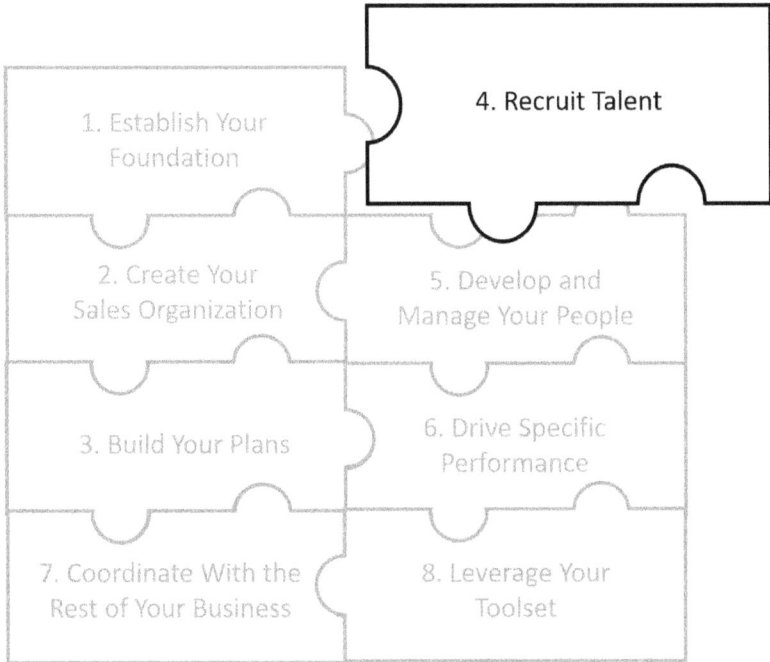

"Great vision without great people is irrelevant."

– Jim Collins, author and consultant

As a sales leader, you may recruit sales talent from within your company or from outside the company. In either case, you need to define the qualities you seek in your hires and learn how to identify candidates who have those qualities. This element discusses the traits you should consider for both sales leaders/managers and sales representatives. For a list of questions you may use when interviewing candidates, see Appendix III – Sample Interview Questions. The list is by no means exhaustive but provides a guide to help you ask questions that delve into how and why candidates manage, sell and lead.

In this element, we examine three areas of recruitment: hiring your sales leader (Chapter 11: Hiring Your Sales Leader), your direct sales reps (Chapter 12: Hiring Your Direct Sales Team) and your indirect sales team (Chapter 13: Hiring Your Channel Sales Team).

Element 4: Recruit Talent

Dynamo*

Dynamo is an internet industry business partner focused on selling business applications on the cloud platforms to small and midsize businesses. Solutions range from families of office tools to artificial intelligence and machine learning systems. The focus of their business is custom applications and related services.

As acceptance of the internet cloud grew rapidly in the mid-2010s, Dynamo struggled to keep pace with their competitors. They had built a solid development team, but they were having difficulty reaching enough customers and prospects to help them apply the new technology to an increasing array of business challenges.

After they had formalized a strategy to attack the market, Dynamo needed to put the right people and resources in place. They identified the skills and expertise they needed. They also mapped the geographies and customer profiles to target. Based on their plan, Dynamo conducted a systematic recruitment effort to identify and hire a sales and marketing team to execute their strategy.

By recruiting the right talent, Dynamo went from a small company to a key partner in the internet business universe in just a few short years.

*Company and individual names have been changed.

Chapter 11: Hiring Your Sales Leader

*"Leadership is unlocking people's potential
to become better."*

— *Bill Bradley, U.S. Senator (1979-1997)*

Your sales leader sets and executes your sales strategy and drives revenue to achieve your company's goals. This person is also responsible for the day-to-day leadership of your sales and marketing teams. This company leader has three essential responsibilities:

- Represent customers and the market on the company's executive management team

- Drive revenue through managing the sales team

- Develop and manage the company's marketing efforts to support revenue generation

Represent Customers and the Market

Sales reps work intimately with specific customers and territories. Your sales leader works across all your sales reps dealing with all your customers in all your markets. Your sales leader is your conduit between your customers and markets and your company. The sales leader is closest to what's going on in your markets: its trends, disruptions, end-user praises and complaints. Your sales leader becomes the voice of your customers and an advocate to drive change on your customers' behalf. At the same time, your sales leader needs to work closely with your other executives to meet the growth needs of the company. Your sales leader must know how market demands may affect company finances, production capability, labor needs and technology requirements. In short, your sales leader must completely understand your business and be fully integrated into the running of the business.

Drive Revenue Through Managing the Sales Team

The sales leader manages and develops the sales team to drive revenue through new customer sales and growth of current customers. In

Element 3: Build Your Plans, we discussed development of the company's strategic plan. The sales leader must put the following in place to execute the sales strategy:

- **Team** – Build a strong, effective sales team that supports achievement of the company goals. We will discuss more about hiring the sales team members later in this element.

- **Training** – Implement a sales training program to develop the necessary skills for the sales team to succeed. Training is discussed further in Element 5: Develop and Manage Your People, Chapter 14: Training.

- **Coaching** – Coach sales team members to improve their sales and business skills and their performance. Include coaching in the areas of the sales process, especially lead and opportunity development, territory planning and management, customer interaction, sales activities, prospecting, closing, and meeting and exceeding goals. Coaching is a development process rather than a directive tool.

- **Processes** – Develop, document and improve the sales processes to ensure that customers and prospects move through the company's sales cycle consistently and effectively. Sales processes include new business development, account management, proposal design and delivery, and closing sales and onboarding customers.

- **Measurements** – Measure and track individual sales representative performance using key performance indicators (KPIs) and performance metrics. We will discuss these concepts further in Element 5: Develop and Manage Your People, Chapter 15: Performance Management. Provide the team with daily feedback on progress toward meeting business goals. Hold team members accountable for individual and team performance.

- **Targets** – Define, assign and communicate business targets for the sales team. Taken together, the sales targets should add up to or exceed the company's business goals, including revenue, margins, product mix, existing customer growth and new customers.

Develop and Manage the Company's Marketing Efforts

In a business-to-business (B2B) company, marketing typically reports into the sales leader. Marketing is responsible for three areas:

- Lead generation

- Market management

- Marketing communications

Let's step through these key areas.

Lead Generation

Marketing generates sales-qualified leads for the sales team. This may be done through internal programs, outsourced programs or a combination of both. For target industries, the marketing team must:

- **Develop ideal customer profiles** that describe what the company's best, most desirable customers look like. These are the customers that generate steady revenue with strong margins. A simple example of an ideal customer profile for a company that sells industrial turbine maintenance services may be: "A mill or manufacturing plant located in the Southeastern United States that generates its own electric power using steam turbines that produce between 25 and 200 megawatts of electricity."

  See Appendix IV - Ideal Customer Profile to review a suggested format for developing an ideal customer profile.

- **Build or buy target prospect lists** of companies that closely match the ideal customer profile. Building lists take time and resources. First, research companies that fit your profile. Next, determine if the target companies are still in business. Finally, identify the key contacts at the companies that your sales team should call on.

- **Source leads** using advertising, email, social media, event marketing and direct calling.

- **Set lead qualification criteria** to differentiate leads likely to close from those that will not. Lead qualification criteria can include company size and location (this is often part of your ideal customer profile), whether the prospect has a specific need that matches your product or solution, or whether the prospect has the resources or money to buy your product or solution. Initially, leads should be "market-qualified" to identify those leads that are promising but not ready for sales. Marketing should "nurture" these leads with email, social media or advertising campaigns to keep them warm until they are ready for direct sales contact. At this point, when the lead is both likely to lead to business and ready for sales to work on, it becomes "sales-qualified."

- **Measure sourcing, campaign and lead effectiveness.** Identify the most effective and efficient ways to generate qualified leads.

Market Management

Market management involves following and comprehensively understanding the market in which your company sells. This means thoroughly understanding your products, prospects, customers and competitors. Competition includes both current competition and trends or technologies that may render your current market offerings obsolete. These are some of the responsibilities of market management:

- Monitor trends and developments in the company's markets. Assess solution offerings, target markets and technologies.

- Identify the total addressable market (TAM) size for each of the company's product lines and markets. Know if the TAM is growing or shrinking. Also, identify how the company may be able to expand its TAM by penetrating adjacent or new markets.

- Identify market trends with respect to the company's product lines and markets. Understand where change is occurring or likely to occur in the near term and longer term. Forecast how market trends will affect TAM and product requirements.

- Develop product solution roadmaps that identify features your future product solutions will incorporate to address market changes and trends.

- Conduct product solution cost analyses and justifications for product solution development and innovation.

- Communicate solution requirements dictated by market changes to the product development team.

Marketing Communications

Marketing communications is incredibly important to your business. This area reinforces your company's brand. It produces and delivers your brand's message consistently across the market. Marketing communications enable the sales team to speak with one voice across all customers, prospects and platforms.

Effective marketing communications include:

- Powerful and effective copy to support sales, marketing and the company's brand, including product and brand positioning and value statements.

- Marketing campaigns that support sales programs, including email, advertising, social media, telephone sales scripts and more.

- Presentations to support sales efforts for key account sales efforts or business reviews and specifically the following presentations:

- o General "About Our Company"

- o Industry-specific "How our products address industry challenges"

- o Solution- or product-specific "Challenges addressed by our products"

- Sales enablement tools that help the sales team sell more effectively, including correspondence templates, advertising, product specification sheets, sales sheets, industry brochures, sales playbooks and proposals.

Hiring the Sales Leader

When recruiting a sales leader, I recommend looking for the following characteristics:

- **Successful selling experience** – Your sales leader needs to know what it takes to sell either business-to-business (B2B) or business-to-consumer (B2C), as appropriate. Your sales leader should become a role model and coach to your sales team, often helping to close major sales. Sales experience helps your sales leader understand both your sales team members and your customers.

- **Sales and marketing management experience** – It's not enough to have been a successful salesperson. Your sales leader also needs to know how to manage people and manage a business unit. Managing a territory is not enough.

- **Command of technology** – In-depth experience using and managing sales technology platforms such as a CRM (Salesforce, HubSpot Sales, Microsoft Dynamics, Zoho) is critical. Today's tools provide sales leaders with the data they need to manage effectively.

- **Knowledge of your company's industry** – This is always a plus but is not always necessary. I'm willing to trade off industry knowledge for strong management experience.

Generally, a smart sales leader can learn the basics of any industry quickly.

- **Education** – I usually look for sales leaders with at least a four-year college degree plus, preferably, an MBA. Candidates with higher levels of education tend to be very motivated, hardworking and achievement-oriented, all excellent qualities for a sales leader.

- **Culture fit** – Make sure your sales leader will fit in with your company's culture. The sales leader must work well with the rest of your company's leadership team, the sales organization and other functions across the company.

Chapter 12: Hiring Your Direct Sales Team

"I hire people brighter than me and I get out of their way."

— Lee Iacocca, Chairman,
Chrysler Corporation (1979-1992)

Your sales team presents the face and voice of your company to your customers. It's especially important to hire the right people for your sales team.

These are the qualities you should look for when hiring your sales reps:

- **Integrity** – Integrity and trust are the foundations of long-term, profitable customer relationships. If you value your brand and customer relationships, you must hire honest sales reps and demand integrity. One lie or misrepresentation can destroy a customer relationship and your trust in the rep in a minute. Therefore, it is imperative that your sales team have the integrity to be honest in all their dealings with you and with your company, customers and prospects.

  I once hired a part-time salesperson to call prospects on behalf of my company. Toward the end of the day, I received a call from a very angry business executive. To reach the decision maker, my salesperson had misrepresented who he was. The executive knew he was lied to and had the courtesy to inform me right away. I apologized sincerely, but we never did business with that prospect. I also fired the sales rep. Since then I have made it a point to check sales candidates' references fully, taking special care to verify their integrity. Can they be trusted?

- **Intelligence** – Sales representatives must be able to think quickly and react to a variety of situations. They must understand their customers' businesses, anticipate customers' needs, adapt their solutions to meet new challenges, and identify and communicate market trends. They must do all this while closing business, driving revenue growth and meeting sales targets. In short, they must be smart, highly intelligent problem solvers.

Intelligence does not necessarily equate with having a college education or advanced degrees, although those can be good leading indicators. I have hired many very smart, very successful sales representatives who did not possess a bachelor's degree. I have also hired very successful sales reps with multiple degrees including MBAs, engineering degrees and PhDs. The key is to hire sales reps who can either understand or quickly learn your business, your markets and your customers.

- **Drive to succeed** – All successful sales representatives I've worked with are driven to succeed. The source of their motivation is usually internal; it's in their DNA and personality. All successful reps do not necessarily have extroverted personalities. Many are not extroverts; introverts can be successful in sales because they tend to listen very well. Sometimes, a person's drive for success comes from outside factors such as the need to support their family or desire for a nice lifestyle.

Whether the drive to succeed is internally sourced or external, the best reps have it. One of the best sales reps I knew at IBM had an incredible drive to succeed, no matter what he did. His drive and passion ultimately took him out of sales. Instead, he became a NASA astronaut and flew on several space shuttle missions. His drive for success took him to heights few others have ever attained.

- **Excellent communication skills** – Successful sales representatives have excellent oral and written communications skills. They use these skills to keep all stakeholders informed, whether customers, managers, the company owner or the board of directors.

Listening, processing, speaking and writing are all important; but first among equals is listening. A strong sales rep will listen closely to what the prospect or customer is telling them or not telling them. The sales rep is listening for needs, objections, opportunities, qualifications, referrals and leads. The best sales reps will listen, probe for better understanding, process what has been said, listen and probe some more. Only after fully understanding the customer's needs and situation will the rep propose a solution that addresses the customer's needs. An untrained rep often tries to sell before the rep has fully listened to the customer. As a result, the rep may miss opportunities to grow a sale or miss information that might help close a sale.

When the sales rep delivers the solution, written and verbal skills are critical. The sales rep must be able to communicate the solution clearly, concisely and accurately, including how and why the solution meets the customer's needs.

Finally, sales reps sell to both external and internal customers. Often, the sales rep must employ their sales and communications skills to gain commitments within the company, whether from senior management, finance or product development. Effective sales reps know who all their customers are.

- **Culture fit** – Pay close attention to how prospective sales representatives will fit within your company's culture. If your company has a highly collaborative culture where plans are developed and agreed on as a team, a sales rep with a closely held, directive style may not be the right choice. Similarly, if you value a hierarchical culture where everyone is expected to follow direction from senior management, a free thinking, "act now, ask for permission later" type of sales rep will also not work out well.

  Look for reps who will work well within your company's culture. Unless, of course, you are looking to change that culture.

- **Appetite for learning** – Top-notch sales representatives recognize that business is constantly changing. They have a need and desire to continually learn and update their skills so they can improve their customers' businesses.

- **Organization and follow-up skills** – Sales representatives are juggling many balls, many commitments simultaneously. It's crucial that your sales reps are well organized to manage leads, prospects, customers and opportunities. In addition, the effective sales rep follows up on all commitments — calls, meetings, references, proposals, quotes, providing information and so on.

- **Basic computer skills** – All sales representatives need basic computer skills. Whether its entering call reports into a customer relationship management (CRM) system, developing and delivering presentations, sending emails, conducting internet research, or creating proposals and letters online, computer skills are essential.

In additional to the qualities listed above, there are other qualities you may need to look for based on the role the sales rep will have in your organization and in the market. These deal with roles and experience levels of the reps you need to hire.

- Entry-level vs. experienced sales reps

- Inside sales vs. field sales reps

- Business development reps vs. key account reps

Entry-Level vs. Experienced Sales Reps

As you build a sales team, you may look to hire a mix of entry-level reps and experienced sales reps. The obvious trade-off between entry level and experienced is cost. You will likely need pay more for experienced sales reps. However, there are other traits you should look for at each level.

Entry-Level Sales Reps

When hiring entry-level sales representatives, I look less for a set of skills or knowledge that they bring to the job and more for strong potential to become a sales professional. I suggest looking for these key traits in entry-level sales representatives:

- **Willingness to learn** – New sales hires must recognize that they are learning a new profession. They must be curious and demonstrate the ability and desire to learn and gain new capabilities. Areas that new sales hires must be willing and able to learn about include:

    o **Sales skills** – Effective sales representatives are developed. They are not born with an innate ability to sell. Some learn faster than others, but all need to be taught. Without sales skills training, whether in a formal program or by working with a seasoned rep with good sales skills, your newly hired sales reps are likely to develop bad habits and not become effective as quickly as possible. I recommend that sales executives and business owners train their sales reps from the start and refresh their training annually.

    o **Markets and customers** – Sales representatives must know their markets and the challenges their customers face. Some of this training comes through formal training, some of it comes through market research and some from other, experienced sales reps. Much of this training comes through speaking with, listening to and interacting with customers and prospects.

    o **Industries** – Entry-level sales representatives must learn about multiple industries. These include the industry in which your company competes (i.e., a network equipment supplier would be in the network communications industry whereas a caterer may be in the hospitality or food services industry). Your sales representatives must also learn about the industries to which they sell. For instance, your sales team may focus on sales to automobile dealers. Or, they may sell to users in the food additives industry. Whatever the case, your sales reps must know the industries into which they are selling.

- o **Products** – Finally, your sales reps need to know your products and their applications. Only by knowing your markets, your customers and their needs, and your products will your sales reps be able to offer valuable solutions to meet their customers' needs.

- **Willingness to be uncomfortable** – Sales often involves putting yourself outside your comfort zone. This is where real learning occurs. If your sales representative is unable or unwilling to venture beyond their comfort zone, they will not grow professionally. Furthermore, they will be unable to sell solutions that stretch their customers' comfort zones. Look for candidates who have taken risks and tried new things.

- **Willingness to put in the time and effort to succeed** – Sales representatives, especially new sales representatives, must put in the time necessary to succeed. When a sales rep is new to sales and new to a territory, the rep must spend many extra hours learning to sell, calling on customers, developing proposals and researching prospects. In short, the sales rep needs to spend many hours laying the groundwork for future success. Look for and hire only those candidates who are willing to put in the necessary hours and who have demonstrated the ability to work hard to succeed.

Experienced Sales Reps

Experienced sales representatives should bring a sales track record to the position that demonstrates they have already learned what it takes to be successful. When interviewing experienced sales representatives, ask questions that probe both their skill level and how they learned their skills. Ask about the challenges and failures they've encountered over the course of their career. Which customers did they not close? Why not? How did they change as a result? Ask about their successes. What contributed to their success? Look for evidence of teamwork, listening to customer needs and creating solutions.

Other traits you should expect to see in experienced sales representatives are:

- **Confidence** – Experienced sales reps are self-confident. They are confident in their sales skills and their ability to follow leads, uncover opportunities, develop solutions and close sales. However, be alert for apparent confidence on the outside that masks underlying insecurities. When interviewing experienced sales reps, ask situational questions that probe their confidence. An example may include "Tell me about a sale that you lost despite being fully confident that you would win it." Or, "Tell me how you prepare yourself mentally going into a sales call with an important (or large new) customer."

- **Solid sales skills** – Experienced sales reps have well-defined sales skills. They should be able to take you through their selling process during an interview. When asked, they should be able to clearly define how they sell, from lead generation through qualification, identifying needs, developing the solution, overcoming objections and ultimately closing. Probe for evidence that the rep's sales skills are current, considering current technologies and tools.

- **Understanding of markets and business** – Experienced sales reps understand and can discuss a wide range of business situations they've faced such as market needs, competition, value proposition, how businesses work (make money), and how to develop and communicate solutions. They can discuss how all these factors work together to create opportunities and drive sales.

- **Willingness to ask for the order** – Experienced sales representatives ask for the order (at the appropriate point).

They do not shy away from asking a customer, or interviewer, for an order or other appropriate commitment/next step. They do not take orders; they make orders happen.

Inside Sales vs. Field Sales Reps

A second consideration in hiring sales reps is whether they will be primarily selling remotely as inside sales reps or face-to-face with your customers as field sales reps. Here again, depending on the rep's role, you will want to look for different personality qualities in the candidates.

Inside Sales Reps

Inside sales is a very tough job for some reps and a dream job for others. On the one hand, inside sales representatives (ISRs) are dealing with a lot of rejection. Particularly when cold calling, over 95% of an inside sales representative's call attempts can result in perceived rejection whether it's no answer, voicemail, a hang up or a direct "no." In addition, ISRs must soldier on hour after hour, day after day.

On the other hand, ISRs can speak with many different people every day. Each contact is an opportunity to win, advance the deal, make a difference and close business. They don't have to travel and are able to interact with more customers in a day than field sales reps deal with in a week.

The best ISRs thrive in this environment. Here are some of the additional qualities you should expect in your inside sales reps:

- **Tenacity** – ISRs hang in there. They continue to call prospects and customers even after they don't reach them the first 2 or 3 times. The best inside sales representatives know that they may need to make 8 to 12 attempts before they speak with a target. Some ISRs motivate themselves with the challenge of reaching their prospects.

- **Positive, "can do" attitude** – Top-tier ISRs have a positive attitude. They have an optimistic outlook and confidence that the next call will be "the one." And if it's not that call, then it will be the one after that.

- **Impervious to rejection, doesn't take it personally** – The best ISRs know that it's not a personal rejection when customers don't answer their calls, don't call them back or simply say "no." More often, there are business reasons the prospect has not said "yes" yet. The effective ISR works to understand the business reason behind the "no" and adapts their sales approach to turn the "no" into a "yes."

- **Warm, reassuring phone voice** – In addition to tenacity and positive attitude, top ISRs also have an attractive "phone voice." Unlike with field sales representatives, prospects cannot see the ISR's professional dress, firm handshake or welcoming smile. Instead, the prospects need to hear it. They need to hear the ISR's professionalism, confidence and smile in their voice. When interviewing ISRs, interview over the phone. Listen for the voice.

Field Sales Reps

Field sales representatives are your company's presence in the marketplace. They are typically calling on your high-value prospects and customers. They are expensive resources and should deliver corresponding value. In addition to the qualities listed above, here's what you should look for in a field sales representative:

- **Capable of being a professional reflection of your company** – The field sales representative is, literally, the face of your company. This rep is the person customers and prospects immediately identify with your company and your brand. You want your field sales representative to reflect the qualities you want your company to project. If your company sells insurance or financial products, you may want your field sales reps to be well-groomed in business suits. If your company sells automotive repair tools, you may prefer your sales reps to look professional but also be ready to climb under a truck to demonstrate a new line of torque wrenches, if necessary. No matter how your sales reps dress, they should always look and be perceived as knowledgeable professionals who can solve your customers' challenges.

- **High energy** – Field sales representatives must engage with customers and prospects all day, every day. This requires physical energy and positive emotional energy. Make sure the field sales representatives you hire have the high energy needed to keep ahead of their customers.

- **Enjoys travel and meeting people** – Field sales representatives should be traveling to visit customers 4 days a week, every week. Fridays or Mondays are usually reserved for planning travel several weeks in advance and doing office-based paperwork. Each day in the field, the sales representative should meet with a minimum of 2 to 3 customers or prospects; more is better depending on the complexity of the sales and length of the sales calls. As a result, field sales representatives should enjoy (or at least tolerate) being on the road travelling. They should also enjoy meeting people as they will be meeting with at least 8 to 12 people every week.

- **Willing to put in long hours and spend time away from home** – Unless your field sales representatives have a local territory, they will spend much of their business week away from home. The field sales reps you hire should be willing to put in that time. Additionally, since regular business hours are prime time for meeting with customers and prospects, your field sales representatives must be willing to put in additional hours outside the prime selling time to complete call reports, enter orders, write proposals and manage administrative tasks.

Since their work is demanding and their value to the company in terms of sales should be high, field sales representatives are normally very well compensated.

Business Development Reps vs. Key Account Managers

The qualities you look for in business development reps (hunters) are also significantly different than those you look for in key account managers (farmers).

Business Development Reps

Business development reps (BDRs) are sales reps who are opening new markets and new customers for your business. They are the key to your long-term growth and expansion, especially for young companies that do not have a strong market presence.

Specific qualities you may look for in a new business development rep include:

- **Brand ambassador** – BDRs should know your company and your market very well. They need to present your company and brand to prospects clearly and succinctly, gaining respect within the market.

- **Creative** – BDRs must be able to develop new ideas and programs to create new business and a better brand. They are constantly alert for new opportunities and challenges that your company's products and services can address.

- **Business acumen** – BDRs need the business acumen to relate to their prospects. They need to be able to understand their prospects' businesses, challenges and needs. Then, they need to be able to know how their products and services can help those businesses, or not.

- **Self-motivated** – BDRs face rejection regularly. They also work in an unstructured environment, seeking out and finding new business. They must believe in themselves and their brand to drive themselves and their business.

- **Engaging personality** – Since BDRs are constantly working to develop new relationships with a wide range of people and personalities, they must be engaging and likeable.

- **Industry experience** – BDRs should have experience specific to your industry, rather than general field sales experience. Specific industry experience helps the BDR to better understand where they can find business opportunities and relate to their prospects' businesses.

- **Team player** – BDRs cannot work alone. They need to work with account sales, marketing and management to efficiently coordinate and drive new business.

- **Integrity** – BDRs have the reputation for doing what they said they would do.

Key Account Manager

A key account is a customer or account that is very important to the success of your business. A key account may be important because of the revenue it delivers each year. It may be an influencer in your market. If so, you must deliver the highest quality products and services so that they will then share their positive experience with other customers. Or it may be a large prospect with the potential to deliver a substantial amount of revenue in the future.

Key account managers (KAMs) usually focus on one key account, but they have a multifaceted role. First, they focus on growing the existing business with the key account. Second, they develop and maintain relationships throughout the account so they can identify new sales opportunities early and develop and close those opportunities to prevent competitors from gaining a foothold in the account. Third, they ensure that the customer receives the service and support necessary to maintain high levels of customer satisfaction throughout the account.

Qualities you may look for in a key account manager include:

- **Leadership** – KAMs lead their customers to see their future with your company's solutions. Key account managers work in their customers' best interests and they lead their customers to realize that using your company's products and services can help them fuel their company's growth.

- **Strong communicator** – KAMs use excellent oral and written communications skills to keep all stakeholders informed (customers, managers, company owner or board of directors).

- **Business acumen** – KAMs understand business and what's important to running and improving the customer's business.

- **Relationship savvy** – KAMs read people and situations. They understand that progress is made through relationships. The most successful ones develop "partnership" relationships with their customers.

- **Results-oriented** – KAMs possess a "get it done" attitude. They have the skills to manage projects, ensuring they are completed on time.

- **Strong appetite for learning** – KAMs are always learning and updating their skills to meet changes in the business and to continue finding new ways to improve their customers' businesses.

The Sales Executive Handbook

Chapter 13: Hiring a Channel Sales Team

"It is much easier to put existing resources to better use than to develop resources where they do not exist."

– George Soros, investor and philanthropist

Some companies supplement their direct sales efforts by developing relationships with channel sales partners. Or, some companies find that it's more efficient to go to market with an indirect or channel sales team. They do not employ a direct sales team to sell their products and solutions. For more information on channel sales, see Element 2: Create Your Sales Organization, Chapter 5: Inside Sales and Field Sales.

There are advantages and disadvantages to going to market with a channel sales team. If you decide to leverage an indirect sales team, I recommend employing a channel sales manager to manage these relationships. A channel sales manager is like a key account manager, but this person focuses solely on channel partners and their unique needs.

Channel Sales Manager

Your channel sales manager recruits and manages your channel sales partners. These are your resellers, distributors, manufacturers' reps and original equipment manufacturers (OEMs) that incorporate your product into their offerings. Channel sales managers are different from direct sales managers because they are managing independent businesses rather than employees. Channel partners may have their own business goals that are not necessarily aligned with your company's goals. Their market approach and sales styles, while influenced by your business's training and direction, may be significantly different from how you approach the market. As a result, when you recruit a channel sales manager, you should look for different traits.

When recruiting a channel sales manager, seek out candidates who display the following:

- **Business acumen** – Channel sales managers must understand what drives their partners' businesses. In addition to understanding the basics of finance — financial statements, accounting, business lending and cash flow among others — channel sales managers must understand what drives business success, what motivates partner managers and owners, and how to grow their partners' businesses.

- **Channel commitment** – They must know how the channel works and why it's important to your business. Your channel manager must be committed to successfully building and growing your sales channels rather than simply viewing channel management as just another sales job.

- **Forward-thinking** – Channel sales managers must be quick-thinking and able to recognize trends. They must be willing and able to share insights across all channel partners, developing best practices for going to market.

- **Relationship-oriented** – Channel sales managers must build business relationships with their channel partners. As such they need to have strong communication skills, both written and verbal, while conveying ideas clearly and concisely. They should also have empathy and the ability to build trust. Finally, the channel sales manager must be able to demonstrate an interest in building and protecting partners' businesses while also building and protecting your company's interests.

- **Flexibility** – Since many success factors are out of the channel sales manager's control, they must have the ability to keep their focus despite unpredictability. At the same time, they must also deliver the results of revenue, EBITDA, or product mix that your company demands.

Channel Sales Partners

Channel sales partners can be original equipment manufacturers (OEMs), sales agents, manufacturers' representatives, distributors and wholesalers, or partners. A successful channel sales manager must understand that each type of channel partner has a role to play in the market that may or may not fit with your company's strategy. Let's look at each one.

Original Equipment Manufacturers (OEMs)

OEMs incorporate your product into their own product, usually branding it as their own. OEMs that add value to the overall solution, such as warranty service, support or functionality, are generally referred to as value-added resellers (VARs).

To illustrate an OEM channel partner relationship, let me tell you about a business I ran that manufactured coin counting machines. These machines were robust, high-speed devices that could count and sort thousands of coins per minute. We sold most of our coin units to retailers and banks that dealt with large volumes of coins daily. However, one customer adapted our coin counting machines and installed them into its own design. The resulting machine could both count coins and currency bills. It could also dispense and accept cashier till drawers to reconcile store registers at each shift change. The result was an even more robust solution that served a market different from our own target market. We had an OEM partner relationship with this customer.

OEMs can be a lucrative primary or secondary market. However, they usually demand consistent product quality over time to meet their own product specifications. They also demand reliable on-time delivery performance to meet their own customers' demand.

Sales Agents

Sales agents can be either exclusive or non-exclusive. Exclusive agents are companies that represent your company and products in a defined territory. They employ their own team of sales representatives to sell in the market. Generally, the exclusive agent will not carry or sell your competitors' products, although they likely carry other company's products that do not compete with yours and may be complementary to your products. In return, your company agrees that it will not contract with other agents to sell your products in the exclusive agent's territory. Territories may be defined as geographies, such as cities, states or countries; industries; or specific customers or targeted prospects.

Non-exclusive agents, as the name implies, represent your company and products, but without an exclusive territory. You may introduce additional agents to the territory as it grows or to provide wider coverage. The drawback of working with a non-exclusive agent is that you may need to pay a higher percentage of sales as a fee or commission to keep the agent's focus on your products. This higher fee is often offset by not having to pay a sales rep's salary and benefits.

Manufacturers' Representatives

Manufacturers' representatives function very much like agents, but they generally work as individuals. They will carry multiple manufacturers' lines that are non-competitive. The challenge involved in working with a manufacturer's rep is that if demand for your product or service is low, the rep will not spend much time trying to generate demand. They will sell the products that represent the greatest income potential for them.

Distributors and Wholesalers

Distributors and wholesalers provide the logistical support, such as warehousing and fulfillment, necessary to extend your products' reach in the market. They also have a set of customers who may need your product to meet their customers' needs. Distributors and wholesalers, like manufacturers' reps, focus their limited marketing resources on those products that sell in volume and generate strong margins.

Partners

Channel partners is a catch-all term that includes all the partner types just discussed. Most frequently, the term "partners" refers to value-added resellers, or VARs, that actively resell a company's products while adding valuable service or functionality.

Element 5: Develop and Manage Your People

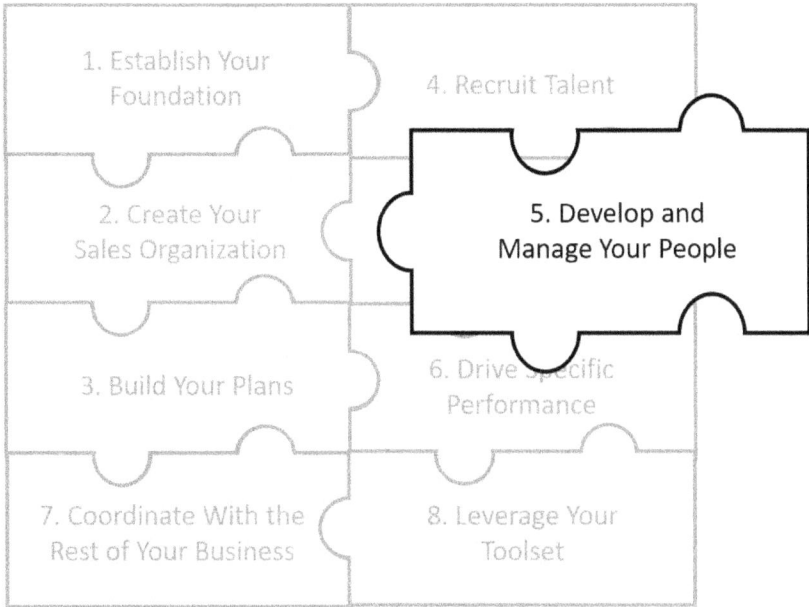

"An organization's ability to learn, and translate that learning into action rapidly, is the ultimate competitive advantage."

> *– Jack Welch, former CEO, General Electric (1981-2001)*

Developing and managing your people has two parts: training and performance management.

Training is essential for building your sales team. It provides them with an understanding of your business and markets. It also helps ensure that your sales team has the skills necessary to sell effectively; the knowledge of the products, services and solutions they are selling; and the ability to effectively use their available sales tools (see Chapter 14: Training).

Through performance management, sales managers communicate goals and expectations. They provide the feedback needed to reinforce activities and behaviors that drive positive results. The performance management process identifies areas where employees can improve their skills and knowledge through training. Performance management can also spot shortcomings in company processes that can be addressed to improve results. Finally, through performance management, sales managers can identify individuals who are unable to contribute to results and should move to other roles, either inside or outside the company (see Chapter 15: Performance Management).

Element 5: Develop and Manage Your People

Winning Networks*

Winning Networks was undergoing a turnaround. After several years of lackluster performance, they had defined their goals, developed a winning strategy and hired key players to augment their sales team. They were ready to execute that strategy.

As they got to work, Winning Networks' management team uncovered a few unaddressed issues. First, not all their sales reps had the skills necessary to sell effectively. Those who did have the skills did not know the market or solutions well enough to shorten their sales cycle. Finally, the truly savvy reps, those who both knew how to sell well and knew their markets and products, were selling what they wanted to sell rather than what the company needed them to sell.

Before Winning Networks could begin to make headway in executing their strategy, they had two areas they needed to address across their sales team. The first area was training. Winning Networks needed to ensure all their sales reps had a base level of sales skills. They needed to know how to sell. They needed to know their products. And, they needed to know their customers and markets so they could deliver solutions their customers valued. The second area was performance management. Winning Networks needed to work with the sales reps to put specific territory plans in place that would support the company's strategy and achieve its goals.

By focusing on developing and managing their people, Winning Networks successfully executed their strategy and profitably grew revenue by double digits in each of the succeeding years.

*Company and individual names have been changed.

Chapter 14: Training

"The only thing worse than training your employees and having them leave is not training them and having them stay."

– Henry Ford, founder, Ford Motor Company

Training is essential for building your sales team. There are five areas to focus on when you train your sales team. Each of these areas is important:

- Company and culture

- Sales skills

- Products

- Markets and competition

- Tools

- Sales leadership

Company and Culture Training

Every successful company has its own culture. Culture is important because it gives your employees a sense of team, a sense of belonging. A strong company culture can help you attract and retain talent. It can also reinforce your brand and make your products more attractive to customers.

A company's culture includes its mission, values, people, attitudes and organization. Training on your company culture starts during the recruiting process, but the most successful companies solidify it in the first days, weeks and months of employment. Company culture training may be conducted by the sales rep's immediate manager or as an ongoing program administered by the human resources department. It should include:

- **Company history** – The company's history explains how the company started and what its original mission was. Teach your employees (not just sales reps) answers to these questions: When was the company started? By whom and why? How did the company grow over the years? What were the important milestones?

- **Mission** – What is the current mission of the company? Is the mission specific? For example, "To deliver low-cost, high-quality heating oil to commercial properties within a 25-mile radius of Danbury, Connecticut." Or, is the mission broad? For example, "To create a safer world through open communications."

- **Values** – The company's values are the guiding tenets of the company. They are long-lasting and important to the company's identity. Examples of company values include "respect for the individual," "positive work-life balance for all associates," or "always deliver best-in-class customer service." Company values are specific to a company and core to its culture.

- **Organization** – How a company is organized, which functional areas are most influential and which associated titles are chosen also reflect a company's culture. Titles such as "Chief Customer Officer" versus "VP of Sales" can reflect cultural norms. Train your team on the company organization, including leadership, department names, key contacts, roles and responsibilities, and location. Include email addresses and other contact information.

- **People** – Certain individuals within a company can have an outsized influence on the company culture. Make sure your team knows who these people are and why they are so important. Also, identify the important contacts the sales representatives need to do their job effectively. This may include managers, sales team peers, administrative support team members and IT help desk. Whenever possible, introduce new hires in person to the people they will need to work with.

- **Attitudes** – Most companies have a cultural vibe or attitude. In some companies, the attitude is highly focused and intense. It may be geared toward driving revenue or opening new accounts. Other companies may be laid back on the surface but have an underlying intensity to succeed. Whatever your company's attitude is, you likely assessed your new hire with that in mind. Just to be certain, be sure to let your sales rep know the company's expectations from the start.

Sales Skills Training

Successful sales efforts demand strong sales skills. Effective selling goes far deeper than the stereotype of the charismatic, fast-talking extrovert. There are many excellent sales training programs to choose from, ranging from Miller-Heiman to Sandler Sales System to IMPAX to many of the custom programs developed for individual companies. What's most important is ensuring that your sales reps have a base set of skills and that they all speak the same sales language. Therefore, it's important for the sales leader to develop a plan (including a timeline with specific people designated as responsible) for training all your sales reps, both entry-level and experienced.

The key competency areas for sales skills that your team should have include:

- **Types of selling** – Your sales team should know the type of selling your company uses to sell to its customers. These are some common types:

    o **Transaction** – A transaction sale usually involves a commodity product and the buying decision is based on price and availability.

    Selling office supplies is a good example of a transaction sale. The products are considered commodities because they are readily available from a variety of suppliers at low prices. The customer places an order online or from a catalog based on the lowest price and availability.

o **Relationship** – A relationship sale is based on the relationship between the buyer and the seller. Often, it is a trust relationship where the buyer will base their decision primarily on price and availability but will give the sales rep "last look" at a deal. Or, the buyer may award the deal because the buyer is comfortable that the product or service will meet all requirements. The buyer may feel confident that the sales rep will deliver on promises made or take care of the customer in the event of unforeseen difficulties in the future.

Selling office supplies can also be a relationship sale if the sales rep has called on the buyer for several years. In this case, if the sales rep has always honored their promises and taken back excess products or satisfactorily settled billing disputes in the past, the buyer will usually go directly to the sales rep for day-to-day office supply orders. When a sales rep has a strong relationship with a buyer, the buyer may decide to go out to bid only for large orders where the price differential may make the savings too large to ignore or orders that are significantly outside the normal course of business.

o **Solution** – Solution sales go beyond providing a product or service at a competitive price and when it's needed, although those criteria are expected. A solution sale involves solving a customer's problem. It tends to be a more complex sale that addresses multiple needs with a complex solution. Solution sales are often seen in the technology space, but they can also apply to selling office supplies.

With office supplies, a solution sale may be one where the buyer is purchasing companywide and for several locations. Many orders are handled by several buyers each day. The solution sales rep recognizes the challenge and cost associated with the buyer's decentralized office supply ordering process. The rep proposes a complete solution where their company will manage the incoming requests for office supplies across the company, fulfill the orders with drop shipments to each location, invoice the company with guaranteed low pricing, and generate a monthly report of orders, products and usage by location.

○ **Partnership** – A partnership sale occurs when the two companies (buyer and seller) in the sale have developed a trusted partner relationship. Unlike a relationship sale, the trust here is between two companies rather than two individuals. Partnership sales are also solution-driven. But rather than reacting to problems as in a solution sale, partners anticipate each other's needs and problems. They work together to implement long-term solutions that benefit both parties.

Extending the solution sale example I just described, a partnership sale occurs when the customer and supplier organizations have developed a high level of trust with each other. As the customer has grown, it has opened locations around the world. To accommodate the customer's burgeoning demand for office supplies, the supplier's sales rep has agreed to implement a "just-in-time" fulfillment process enabled by having stocked warehouses within 100 miles of each customer location that has more than 1,500 employees. The supplier guarantees that prices will be within 3% of the lowest average competitive price and delivery will be within 24 hours. In return, the customer agrees to purchase 90% of its office supplies from the supplier with a minimum annual spend and provide a monthly purchase forecast. Both companies benefit from the partnership relationship and both have commitments to the other.

- **Sales cycles and buying cycles** – The sales cycle refers to the steps through which a sale progresses. The buying cycle refers to the steps through which the buyers make their decision to purchase. Effective sales reps weave their sales cycle into the buying cycle, sometimes following the buyer, other times leading the buyer. The typical sales cycle steps are: uncover needs, create urgency, define solution, make a proposal, and implement or close. The typical buying cycle steps are: identify need, decide to act, evaluate options, review internally and approve purchase. See Element 1: Establish Your Foundation, Chapter 2: Strategy for more on sales cycles and buying cycles.

- **Prospecting and lead management** – Prospecting and lead management go together. In larger companies, marketing may handle these functions; in smaller companies, the sales reps do. Prospecting is the challenging process of finding new customers. Lead management is the process by which leads are followed up on, qualified and nurtured until they are ready to be actively sold. Leads are the lifeblood of sales since they present opportunities for future sales.

  - **Follow-up** – Too often sales representatives do not follow up on leads in a timely manner. You must put a process in place to encourage and help reps follow up on leads and teach your sales team to execute against that process. Leads that are not followed up on or that are followed up on after too much time has passed represent wasted marketing dollars and lost revenue.

  - **Qualification** – Not all leads are equal. Train your sales representatives to qualify leads against your specific buying criteria. These buying criteria determine if the lead is for an opportunity where the prospect is ready, willing and able to buy your product or service.

- o **Nurturing** – Many leads are opportunities, but the prospect is not yet ready to buy. The prospect may be gathering information in advance of a purchase. Perhaps the prospect is qualifying vendors. Or, the prospect could just be interested in knowing more about a market or technology. There are many reasons why a prospect may not be ready to buy yet. In these cases, your company needs to nurture the lead until the prospect is ready to buy. Lead nurturing may be done by the sales team or the marketing team. Either way, you must train your sales representatives on how to manage leads for prospects that are not yet ready to buy.

- **Territory and account planning** – Every territory and key account should have an annual plan to meet or exceed its sales targets. Sales reps should review their plans quarterly with management and update the plans as conditions change. Many sales representatives, including experienced sale reps, either do not know how to write plans or they simply fail to do so. Territory and account planning should be included in your sales training program. See Element 3: Build Your Plans, Chapter 10: Creating Territory Plans for more information on territory and account planning.

- **Account management** – Train your sales reps on how your company manages account relationships, from pre-sale through the sales process and then post-sale. Account management includes customer service, active sales management (especially for key accounts), maintenance and support.

- **Opportunity management and sales pipeline management** – Training should include how to manage opportunities in the sales pipeline to ensure they convert to sales. Also, pipeline management is a skill whereby the sales representatives ensure they have opportunities in every stage of the sales cycle so that revenue flows at an even pace throughout the year.

- **Sales calls** – Train your sales representatives, especially new sales reps, on how to conduct sales calls. Include identifying differences in calls at different levels within a customer's organization, setting a purpose for a call, structuring a call and asking for the order. Sales calls can vary based on the size and complexity of the sale and where the sale is in the sales cycle.

  - o **Anatomy of a sales call** – Your reps need to know how to structure a sales call. Common parts of the sales call may include introduction and rapport building, questioning for needs, presentation of a solution, overcoming objections, trial close, negotiation and closing. Not all sales calls will include all parts of this structure.

  - o **Phone-based calls** – Your reps need to know how to set up a phone-based sales call. Train them on how to define the structure of the call and emphasize how to address objections and overcome rejection. Train your sales representatives how to use a telephone script, how to practice the script and how to personalize it so they own it themselves.

  - o **In-person, face-to-face calls** – Train your sales reps how to structure sales calls, define the purpose of the call, follow the steps of the sales call, and produce and deliver effective presentations for use during calls.

- **Cross-selling and upselling** – Train your sales reps how to get the most from a selling opportunity, including selling complementary products and additional features.

- **Overcoming objections and negotiation** – Customers often look for reasons not to buy. Train your sales reps how to overcome obstacles to closing the sale. Teach them to negotiate terms and conditions that go beyond price and availability.

- **Closing** – Many sales reps are reluctant to ask for the order. Train your sales reps to identify buying signals and ask for the order.

Product Training

Knowing your products and how they benefit your customers is vitally important. Teach your sales reps about both your products and your competitors' products. Show them the differences. Train them to identify the situations where your products or services can solve problems for your customers and prospects. Product training emphasizes features and benefits, but it also includes market positioning, competitive advantages and customer needs. Train your sales reps to know how your products solve the business problems your customers face.

Markets and Competition Training

Sales reps must know both the markets into which they are selling and the competitors they will encounter. Markets are important for the sales reps to understand who customer and prospects are and where they are located. Questions they must be able to answer include:

- How large is my market? Is it growing or shrinking?

- What does my ideal customer look like?

- Why do customers buy my products or services? Why do they buy my competitors' products or services?

In addition, your sales reps must know who their competition is and how to beat the competition.

- How big are my competitors?

- How do my competitors sell to their customers?

- What advantages do my competitors have over my company and products?

- What advantages does my company have over my competitors?

- How can I avoid competition?

- What are the market's perspectives on my company and on my competitors?

Tools Training

Your sales representatives will use many tools to make themselves, the company and their customers more efficient. Don't assume they already know how to use them. Train your sales representatives on how to use the tools in the most efficient way you need and want them to use the tools.

Examples of tools include your customer relationship management (CRM) system, order processing and tracking systems, and technology tools such as computers and various types of software (Microsoft Office or Google Google Workspace, for example). If you have proposal templates and prepared presentations, your sales reps should know how to access them and how to use them. Also, make sure your sales reps are trained on all types of demonstration equipment. For more information on sales tools, see Element 8: Leverage Your Toolset, Chapter 20: Other Important Tools.

Sales Leadership Training

Training your sales team is important. Equally important, if not more so, is training your sales leader. Too often, successful sales representatives are promoted to lead their peers with the expectation that since they have been successful selling in the field, they will continue their success by showing their peers how to sell. Sometimes this works; more often it does not.

Selling and managing a sales team require different skill sets. Sales representatives are responsible for "selling," which includes determining their own actions or following a set plan of actions developed for their team. They carry responsibility for the success of their own sales efforts. Sales representatives focus on their own territory and customers.

On the other hand, sales leaders are responsible for "managing" a team of sales reps and helping them to be successful. They must focus on developing the skills and talents of others. Sales leaders work to drive success outwardly across multiple territories and across a range of customers. They must also manage internally across the company to ensure that the company strategy is clear and appropriate. Sales leaders must communicate clearly with operations, production, human resources, finance and all the other functional areas of the company.

Do not sell your company short by assuming that your successful sales representative will become a successful sales leader without management training. Invest in training your sales leader to ensure they have the skills needed to build and manage an effective sales team. This book is a good start. Make sure your sales leader understands all the concepts contained in this book. Also invest in leadership and management training. Just a few areas to cover and develop include:

- Coaching and mentoring

- Strategy implementation and execution

- Decision making

- Managing and leading change

- Delegation and working through others

- Collaboration

- Business planning

Management and leadership training are available from many sources including leading business schools such as Harvard Business School, Stanford Graduate School of Business, Wharton and Columbia University Business School. There are also many independent programs available that are classroom-based, self-paced and online. Before investing in a program, do your homework. Research the programs that fit your needs, schedule and budget. Reputable programs with referenceable track records are your best bet.

Training Frequency

Training is not a one-time, classroom-based investment. To be effective, you need to make training part of your sales culture by adding at least two additional components. First is reinforcement. Classroom or online training introduce concepts and skills at a conceptual level. However, for those skills to take root and become habits, your reps need to reinforce their skills through implementation and practice in the days, weeks and months following the formal training. If you invest in a training program delivered by an outside vendor, choose a program that reinforces skills over time. The result will be a better-trained, more effective sales team.

Second, provide ongoing training. Set up a schedule that provides regular training for your sales team each year. Designate someone to be responsible for the training.

The following page shows an example of a sales training schedule.

The best sales organizations are learning organizations where training is ongoing, providing your sales team with a continuous improvement process.

Sample Annual Sales Training Schedule

- January – Sales kick-off meeting (3-4 days)
    - Review of company goals and values
    - Introduce company and sales strategy for the year
    - 1 day of new product training/half day of existing product training
    - Half day of sales skills training
    - Half day of sales tools training
- Quarterly webinars – April and October
    - Tools training – New features, refresh of current tools
    - Product training – Focus on one or two key products
    - Skills – Review one or two key skills
- Midyear
    - New product announcements and training
    - Tools reinforcement
    - 1 day of sales skills

Chapter 15: Performance Management

"The greatest leader is not necessarily the one who does the greatest things. He is the one that gets the people to do the greatest things."

– Ronald Reagan, 40ᵗʰ U.S. President

It's simply not enough to hire the right people and ensure they are trained. To get your sales team to generate the best results, you need to manage their performance. This means setting expectations, defining goals, measuring progress and providing feedback. There are three excellent tools you can use to ensure this is done:

- Territory plans for your sales team

- Development plans for every employee, including the sales team

- Performance improvement plans

This chapter focuses on sales reps' performance management, but these tools can be used to manage performance of employees in marketing or any area of the company.

Territory Plans

As discussed extensively in Element 3: Build Your Plans, Chapter 10: Creating Territory Plans, well-defined territory plans directly relate to how a sales representative or sales team will achieve their business goals. Business goals include revenue and margin quotas, account expansion, new customers closed, product sales, and product mix, to name a few. In short, the business goals for a sales rep contribute directly to the overall success of the company. A territory plan or account plan (when dealing with a key customer account) is a plan specific to that territory or account. It presents a path to achieve the goals assigned to that territory or account. The territory plan is not specific to a particular sales rep. If, during the year, the sales representative assigned to a territory changes, the new sales rep should be able to continue execution of the territory plan and achieve their assigned goals.

Development Plans

A development plan is specific to each sales representative. It incorporates business and professional goals for a defined period. For most employees this is one year, although it does not have to coincide with the calendar year. In fact, if you have several sales reps, you will likely find the workload easier if you spread development review dates across the year. The initial development plan period for a new sales rep is often six months to provide more immediate feedback while the sales rep is adjusting to becoming part of the team.

In a development plan, you set individual goals for the sales rep. I break the goals into two sections: company and business goals and professional development goals. I recommend setting three goals for each section and making the goals personal for each employee. Goals should be reasonably attainable, meaning the employee should have to work hard to reach the goals, but also see a path to getting there. Goals should be neither too easy to reach nor beyond reasonable reach. Above all, goals must be clearly defined and quantified. And the employee must be able to determine whether they have reached their goals or not.

Company goals relate to achieving business objectives. For a sales representative, company goals may relate to revenue or gross margin quota achievement, mix of products sold, or number of new customers closed that deliver a minimum revenue amount. Professional development goals relate to the individual's career development and are developed jointly by the manager and sales rep. Examples of professional development goals include attending sales skills training, mentoring a new sales rep, improving presentation skills or learning more about another business function such as finance, human resources or production.

Examples of Development Plan Goals

	Too Broad	Clearly Defined and Quantifiable
Company and Business **(Developed by manager and reviewed with sales rep)**	• Meet or exceed quota	• Generate a minimum of $2.5 million of sales revenue from May 2020 through April 2021
	• Sell more widgets	• Sell 200 units of the new model widgets over the next 12 months
	• Close more new customer accounts	• Close 24 new customers that we have not done business with previously • Each new customer must generate at least $10,000 of sales revenue
Professional Development **(Jointly developed by manager and sales rep)**	• Improve your sales skills	• Attend the week-long "Advanced Selling" training course • Present a summary of what you learned to the sales team in a 20-minute program

Too Broad	Clearly Defined and Quantifiable
• Mentor Sally Jones	• Work with Sally Jones as a mentor • Take her on 2 sales calls every month • Meet with her weekly to develop her sales skills
• Deliver better presentations	• Spend 2 hours each month working with your manager to improve your presentation skills • Focus on both developing and delivering presentations of 15 to 30 minutes • Deliver two presentations to the full sales team in the next 12 months
• Learn more about how our business works	• Over the next 12 months, spend 1 hour each month with a VP (or designate) of a functional area outside sales (minimum 4 areas). • Learn what each function does to contribute to the company's success. • After each meeting, spend 20 minutes with your manager discussing what you learned.

Over the course of the plan period, usually 6 or 12 months, measure your rep's performance against their development plan. Make notations of what has been accomplished, has been done well and needs improvement. Have regular weekly or monthly conversations with your rep to share your observations. When the time comes for a formal review of your rep's development, there should be no surprises as you have both discussed progress over the course of the plan period.

During the formal review, which you conduct at the end of the plan period, provide your rep with a development rating, documentation that supports your rating and suggested changes to the rep's work habits to improve their performance. Everything should be in writing with a copy to the rep and another copy to the rep's personnel file.

Keep ratings simple and understandable. When I worked for IBM, we used a simple 1 to 5 scale that corresponded as follows:

1. Far exceeds expectations

2. Consistently exceeds expectations

3. Meets expectations and occasionally exceeds expectations

4. Meets expectations

5. Fails to meet expectations

For each goal, the employee was rated on the 1 to 5 scale. Managers also assigned a weight to each goal relative to its importance to the business and employee. Based on the goal ratings and associated weights, each employee earned an overall performance rating ranging from 1 to 5. Employees who were regularly rated a 1 or 2 earned higher salary increases and faster promotions. Employees who were rated less than 4 were moved out of the company.

Some companies expand the performance assessment to incorporate feedback from a wider group than just the manager and employee. These reviews, often referred to as 360-degree reviews, solicit input from coworkers with whom the employee interacts, other managers and, sometimes, customers.

Following the formal development review, you and your employee should create a new development plan for the next 6 to 12 months.

Performance Improvement Plans (PIP)

Over the course of the plan period, if you determine that a rep's performance is below your expectations, you should consider placing the rep on a performance improvement plan (PIP). A performance improvement plan is like a development plan, but it identifies more specific goals and implements daily or weekly activity reviews. As the term suggests, this plan charts a corrective path that the rep needs to follow with specific milestones they must attain to change their performance and get back to making positive contributions to your team.

The performance improvement plan should be used as a tool to improve the rep's performance, not as a tool to document deficiencies in anticipation of terminating the rep's employment with the company. If you have determined that the rep's performance cannot be improved, then you are better off terminating their employment immediately rather than wasting time and resources involved in executing a performance improvement plan. Justification for a rep's termination should have been documented over the course of the original development plan period.

Structure of a Performance Improvement Plan

You should document all performance improvement plans (PIPs). I recommend this structure for the PIP:

- **Purpose** – State the reason why you are placing the rep on the PIP. Also state the objectives of the plan. Here's an example:

  [Rep's name], as we have discussed, you are not meeting the company's quota and performance standards. I am, therefore, presenting you with this performance improvement plan to help you reestablish your sales success at this company.

The purpose of this performance improvement plan is to:

1. Identify area(s) where you are not meeting acceptable performance standards

2. Clearly define performance objectives that will lead to success

3. Establish a course of action to help you bring your performance up to an acceptable level.

- **Performance History** – Include a brief history of the rep's performance that led to placing the rep on a PIP. Wherever possible, use clear data such as number of deals closed, revenue generated, attainment versus quota or new accounts opened. You may also present target activity levels for the activities that lead to sales success, including number of calls made, number of quotes or proposals presented, or number of leads generated. Compare the rep's activity levels with the target levels associated with success.

- **Performance Success Objectives** – Present the minimum activity and results levels that the rep would need to meet to generate success.

- **Performance Improvement Plan** – Lay out the action plan that the rep will need to follow to improve their performance. The plan should include metrics so that the rep and manager can both measure progress. It should also identify the habits the rep should develop to generate success. Finally, the action plan should present the results the rep should deliver and the time frame for generating the results.

- **Time frame** – The PIP needs to clearly present the time frame in which the rep must improve performance and deliver results. Time frames can range from 1 to 2 weeks for transaction-oriented sales to 60 to 90 days for complex sales. Time frames can be extended or shortened based on progress.

However, you need to ensure they are realistic within your environment.

- **Review Timetable** – Present a schedule for the rep and manager to review activities and results associated with the PIP. Generally, PIP reviews should be conducted at least weekly for plans with a 2- to 3-month time frame and twice weekly (or even daily) for shorter time frames.

- **Documentation** – Following each review, the manager should document discussions and progress, sharing observations with the rep.

- **Consequences** – The PIP should clearly state the consequences for the rep if the performance success objectives are not met. Consequences may range from demotion to reassignment to termination of employment. Be realistic about the consequences and stick to them if performance remains unacceptable.

Finally, both the rep and manager should sign the PIP to indicate that they are each committed to improving performance and delivering success.

Element 6: Drive Specific Performance

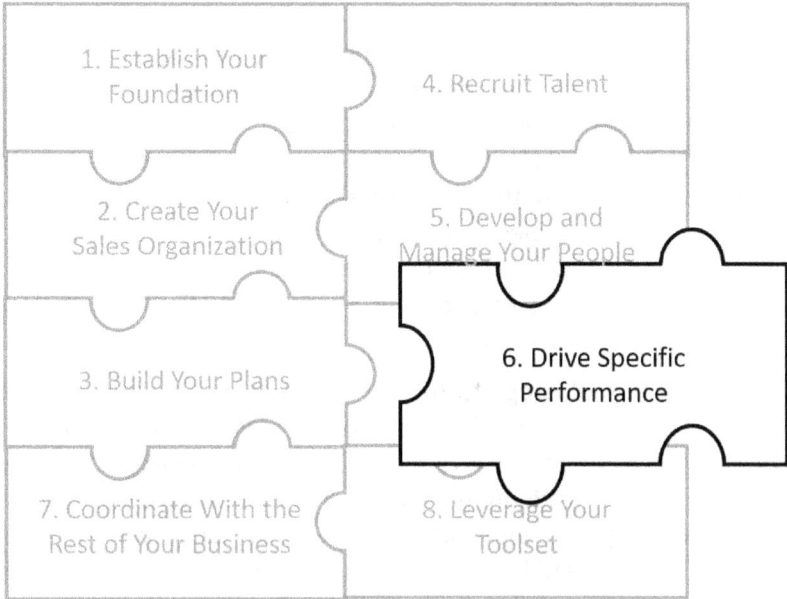

"Vision without action is a daydream.
Action without vision is a nightmare."

– Japanese Proverb

To drive specific sales performance, you need motivation and accountability. Motivate your sales teams with both monetary incentives and non-monetary rewards (see Chapter 16: Motivation and Chapter 17: Performance Incentives). Hold your team accountable for taking actions to meet or exceed goals and expectations (see Chapter 18: Accountability).

Element 6: Drive Specific Performance

Capital Equipment Leasing*

Capital Equipment Leasing (CEL) provided equipment lease financing to medium-size and large corporations across the United States. Mike was responsible for CEL's leasing sales for Southern California. His territory ranged from California's border with Mexico north to Santa Barbara and from the Pacific Ocean to the Nevada and Arizona borders. It included the major cities of Los Angeles and San Diego. Taken on its own, Southern California ranks as one of the world's largest economies. However, Mike was floundering. Despite long hours and hard work, Mike was not closing many new customers or deals.

Mike's manager took steps to turn his performance around. First, she communicated specific goals for Mike to work towards. Next, they agreed to focus Mike's efforts to achieve the goals. Rather than going after every opportunity that Mike identified, they agreed that Mike would focus only on the 50 largest companies in Southern California. This was counterintuitive since Mike had been clamoring for more territory so that he could look for more opportunities. But focusing on specific performance became a priority. Next, they put specific account plans in place for each of the 50 companies. Mike now knew what he needed to achieve, where he needed to focus his efforts and what actions he needed to take.

With his manager helping Mike to drive specific performance, Mike closed more leases within three months than he closed in the previous year.

*Company and individual names have been changed.

Chapter 16: Motivation

"If you are working on something that you really care about,
you don't have to be pushed. The vision pulls you."

— *Steve Jobs, Apple co-founder*

"Not everything that can be counted counts and
not everything that counts can be counted."

— *Albert Einstein, theoretical physicist*

People can be driven by two different types of motivation, intrinsic and extrinsic. Intrinsic motivation is an internal drive. A person acts based on "intrinsic" motivations when they find an activity enjoyable or they see it as an opportunity to satisfy a passion or curiosity, or to grow as an individual. When a person acts based on "extrinsic" motivations, they do so because they want to earn an external reward or avoid a punishment.

Intrinsic vs. Extrinsic Motivation

Sales reps, like everyone, are also driven by intrinsic and extrinsic motivations. Sales reps may sell because they enjoy the competition that comes with sales. Or, they may be driven to help businesses solve problems that their product or offering addresses. Or, they may simply like meeting people and learning about their businesses. These may all be classified as intrinsic motivations.

To focus sales reps to act in specific ways that benefit your company, you may offer extrinsic motivations. These may include commissions tied to goals, bonuses for specific achievements, recognition for jobs well done or, on the flip side, penalties for failure to deliver results.

So, what are the main differences with respect to driving performance?

Intrinsic motivation tends to be long-lasting. It's tied to the individual's personality. Every healthy person has self-fulfillment needs that drive them. They must be continually satisfied. These needs may range from feeling good about oneself through simple enjoyment to getting a sense of accomplishment by acting with a sense of purpose. Personal growth, curiosity, learning and following one's passion are also examples of intrinsic motivation.

Extrinsic motivation, on the other hand, tends to be short-term. A sales rep is driven to attain a reward because the reward (or punishment) leads the rep to be able to satisfy other needs. For example, a rep may work hard to get a large commission, not for the money itself, but for what the money can buy. In some cases, it may be a new car (enjoyment of driving); in others, it may be more or better food on the table; in still others, it may be a way of keeping score against other reps (the satisfaction of being recognized as the best). However, once the underlying need is met, the value of the reward diminishes unless a new need that the reward can address takes its place.

Intrinsic Motivation

Given that intrinsic motivation is internally generated and driven by the love of the job or task itself, and differs across individuals, it begs a question. How can a manager tap into the intrinsic motivation of sales reps?

The answer to this question may be explained by the Job Characteristics Model. This model, developed in 1976 and updated in 1980 by organizational psychologists J. Richard Hackman and Greg R. Oldman, identified three core job characteristics that keep people engaged and doing well:

- **Skill variety** – Individuals find jobs more meaningful when the jobs have a wide range of activities requiring several different skills and abilities.

- **Task identity** – Jobs are more meaningful when the individual performing the jobs completes a whole segment of work from beginning to end. Assembly line production, where individuals perform the same task over and over, is the antithesis of task identity. To provide individuals with a sense of task identity, some high-end automakers put together teams who assemble an entire vehicle rather than individual specialists who perform only one specific activity.

- **Task significance** – Individuals find jobs meaningful when they perceive that their work substantially improves the well-being of others. In other words, people like to make a positive impact on other people.

These core characteristics can be multiplied or diminished by two additional characteristics:

- **Autonomy** – The degree to which a person has the freedom and independence to determine a plan for how they will do a job and the freedom to execute the plan. With greater autonomy comes greater responsibility and satisfaction of achievement. Autonomy also brings greater risks in the event of failure.

- **Feedback** – The degree to which the person receives clear and timely feedback on performance effectiveness. Feedback can come from peers and management, or it may come from seeing or experiencing the results of the person's own actions.

Building on the Job Characteristics Model, organizational psychologist David Burkus posits that you can strengthen intrinsic motivation within your sales reps by addressing the following questions:

- How can we provide more autonomy?

- How can we put systems in place to increase feedback?

- What can we do to increase the variety of tasks worked on?

- How can we make people see the end result of their work?

- How can we help people see that their work positively affects people?

(Burkus 2020, davidburkus.com, "Extrinsic Vs Intrinsic Motivation at Work")

When applied to management of our sales teams, each of these questions helps us to create an environment in which sales reps can become more engaged in selling.

For the sales executive, the challenge becomes "How do you develop a sales team whose intrinsic motivation matches the activities associated with selling?"

There are three paths to achieving that objective. You can hire people into your sales positions who are already intrinsically motivated to sell. You can develop new sales reps to become professionals who are passionate about selling. Or you can do both.

To hire people who are intrinsically motivated to sell, you must listen for and observe traits that are consistent with a passion for selling during the interview process. These traits may include wanting to meet new people, a desire to solve problems, attentive listening skills or a passion for learning. These are just a few of many traits that may signal a passion for selling.

To develop a passion for sales, training and feedback are important. People generally enjoy doing activities that they do well and are confident in doing. A direct path to doing things well and with confidence is through training. Invest in training your sales reps with solid sales skills. Give them the feedback they need to continually improve. As they become experienced sales reps and learn to sell successfully, they are likely to develop a passion for selling.

Ideally, your sales organization should both hire for success and provide the training and feedback needed to sell effectively. This combination can produce an extraordinarily successful sales team that wants to sell and grow their customers.

Extrinsic Motivation

While it's great to have a sales team of intrinsically motivated reps, there are times when extrinsic rewards can deliver immediate focus on the activities necessary to achieve your goals. Use these rewards to direct performance.

Extrinsic motivation can be in the form of either a "carrot" or a "stick." A carrot approach offers a desirable reward such as money or recognition to drive positive behavior. The carrot can drive high levels of short-term performance. It may, for the company offering the reward, be the price of admission or the ante to play the game. An example of such a "carrot" is salary. The company needs to pay a competitive salary to attract or retain good sales representatives. The carrot may also be viewed by the sales reps as a method of keeping score versus other team members or colleagues outside the company.

The stick approach to extrinsic motivation works on negative incentives. It threatens a penalty for failure to act in a desired manner or failure to deliver desired results. As an example of a stick motivation, a sales manager might take away good accounts or reduce territory if the sales rep does not meet quota.

There are four major drawbacks to using a "stick" to drive motivation:

- **Lower sales performance** – Demotivated sales reps can suffer a decrease in productivity, by as much as 25% or more according to some studies.

- **Physical and emotional harm** – The stress created by negative incentives can cause physical harm such as ulcers or migraines and emotional harm including anxiety and depression.

- **Creates a hostile work environment** – Employees become defensive and resentful, evade responsibilities and avoid the manager.

- **Promotes a negative attitude** – This is a real momentum killer as reps become reactive (i.e., defensive) and looking to avoid failure, rather than being proactive and looking to drive success.

Examples of positive extrinsic motivators include:

- Base salary

- Benefits – health, disability and life insurance

- Car allowance

- Commissions

- Raises

- Preferred parking spaces (not recommended for field sales reps who should not be spending much time at the office)

- Bonuses and awards

- Sales contests

- Recognition events and trips

- Promotions

- Recognition plaques

- "Employee of the month"

Motivating Sales Reps Beyond Money

Sales rep recognition can go a long way beyond cash compensation. In addition to paying cash, sales representatives are also motivated by recognition before their peers and family. There are several ways you can leverage this:

- **Recognize your sales representatives' achievements before their peers.** You may decide to hold monthly sales meetings or quarterly all-company meetings. At these events, call out your high achievers and present them with a token of recognition. The token can be as simple as a handshake for a job well done or more complex ranging from gift certificates for dinner to plaques to parking spaces in premium locations. The key is to provide recognition that is commensurate with the level of achievement and to do so publicly.

Another way you can recognize sales reps is through sales contests. In a sales contest, you set the goal and time frame. Then, over the course of the contest, post results where everyone can see their (and everyone else's) progress to the goal. You may decide to set minimum qualifying levels of achievement to win an award. At the end of the contest, publicly present the award whether it's a pat on the back, a premium item such as a new Yeti cooler, or a preferred parking space in the company lot.

- **Recognize your top sales representatives' achievements before their families or partners.** This recognition can be done by providing your sales representatives with a "night on the town," perhaps dinner and a show, that they can share with a significant other. Similarly, you may offer recognition events that include partners/spouses or send a gift basket to their home so that the entire family can know about your sales rep's success and join in enjoying the award. The benefit of this type of award is that the family becomes part of your team as well.

Recognition can go a long way toward motivating your sales team. The key is to offer recognition perks that are highly valued by the recipient but have costs that are well below the value they deliver. Also, whenever possible, tie the recognition to the achievement. An award of a month's worth of hotel upgrades will be more meaningful to your road warrior than a premium reserved space in the company parking lot. Similarly, a pair of tickets to see the hometown baseball team play may be more appropriate award for a sales team competition than tickets to a movie that is enjoyed alone.

Chapter 17: Performance Incentives

"Goals allow you to control the direction
of change in your favor."

– Brian Tracy, author and speaker

Motivation via Sales Compensation

For most sales reps, compensation is the most important vehicle for communicating your sales expectations. If your compensation plan is developed and aligned with achievement of your company's strategic goals, it will allow you to:

1. Drive achievement of company goals

2. Enable your sales team to realize their personal and professional goals

3. Attract and retain top sales representatives

Simply paying your sales representatives a percentage of the revenue or gross margin they deliver may achieve the second and third of the compensation plan purposes, but it will not drive achievement of the company's goals. Most sales reps will spend their time and resources where 1) they will make the most commissions and 2) it's easiest for them to sell. As a result, sales reps become motivated to:

- Sell on price, dropping your sales price, rather than selling on the value your solution provides

- Sell to existing customers rather than expanding your market footprint

- Sell lower margin or commodity products rather than higher margin, new products that represent your company's future

Let's look at each of the three compensation plan purposes.

1 – Drive Achievement of Company Goals

Generally, there are four categories of company goals that you can drive through a well-designed sales compensation plan — financial, customer, product and market. Design your sales compensation plan to focus your sales team on achieving three or four of these categories.

Financial Goals

Financial goals are the most common goals associated with sales — specifically, revenue and gross margin goals. The most common way to incorporate your revenue and gross margin goals into a commission plan is to set quotas equal to the goals and pay a commission for every dollar generated. Slightly more sophisticated plans may add commission accelerators to pay a higher percentage for all business generated over quota. Implemented by themselves, financial incentives and measurements can effectively drive revenue and margin, but they do not allow you to steer efforts to realize other company goals. For that, you need to incorporate these other categories into your sales compensation plan.

Customer Goals

Usually, companies have three customer goals: retain and grow existing customers, open new customers and land or expand specific, targeted customers.

Retain and grow existing customers. When trying to retain and grow existing customers, you have multiple options. First, you might set a quota for your existing accounts that represents year-over-year growth. Based on the quota, you may pay a percentage of revenue for all business attained before reaching quota and a higher percentage for business attained over quota. Quotas can be set territory-wide (most common) or they may be set individually for each account with territory-wide thresholds. Individual account quotas are less common because tracking them requires more administrative work, but they do ensure that sales reps focus on all their accounts rather than simply the top accounts.

A second option is to use tiered commissions. Tiered commission levels are not limited to two levels, under quota and over quota. You can implement multiple levels to drive desired performance. For instance, you may use sales accelerators where you increase the commission rate as milestones are attained. For example, a sales accelerator might pay 1% of revenue up to 90% of quota, 1.5% between 90% and 100%, 3% over 100%, and 5% over 115%. The key is to set up a program that works within your company's financial structure and focuses the rep on the company's sales goal.

A third option is to pay commissions only based on the growth of a territory. Under this scenario, the sales rep earns commissions for net additional revenue from a customer but loses commissions if the customer produces less revenue than they had in prior years.

Open new customers. Opening new customers as a commission goal requires a similar approach but with a different focus. With new accounts, you may also apply a quota or target, but instead of setting a revenue quota, you may set a quota on the number of new accounts. The new account quota may also specify that new accounts must meet a minimum standard such as at least $10,000 of revenue in the first year or within 3 months of the initial order. In this way, you focus your sales rep on closing new accounts that are of a minimum size and on driving additional revenue from new accounts.

Another way to focus your sales representatives on closing new accounts is to put a bonus on each new account they close. Like new account quotas, you need to define what accounts qualify for the bonus. For example, you may define a new account as any account that has not done business with your company in the last 3 years and generates at least $20,000 of revenue in the current plan year. You can then set bonuses such as $50 for each new account or $250 for each set of five new accounts.

Land targeted customers. For targeted customers, you may decide to offer a bonus for penetrating a targeted account, set quotas for revenue achievements within the targeted accounts, or pay higher commission rates for sales to targeted accounts. Some companies use a combination of all three techniques to drive the desired results.

Product Goals

Often, a company may need to focus its sales team on selling new or different products. The reasons can vary. Sometimes, the company has announced a new product that is not yet accepted in the market. As a result, the reps are not likely to spend a lot of their selling time focused on the new product since it is harder to sell and earned commissions are likely to be low. Other times, the company needs to change the mix of products they sell to emphasize products that will drive future growth. Or, the company may want to shift reps to selling more high-price, high-margin products if the reps are currently focused on low-price easy sales.

As shown with customer goals, you can also focus your sales team on your product goals using a combination of quotas with commission rate accelerators, variable commission rates on different products and bonuses for specific product sales.

Market Goals

You can use the compensation plan to drive market or industry penetration, too. Often, companies have a goal to expand their market presence into new geographies, new industries or new customer demographics. Geographic expansion may be as simple as developing new customers in an adjacent region or as complex as starting international operations. Moving into new industries is often a growth strategy, as your product solutions may be applicable to industries related to those your current customers are in. Expanding customer demographics may mean that your company is targeting larger customers than those you have traditionally done business with.

As demonstrated above with customers and products, you can place higher commission rates on transactions closed in markets you have targeted for entry. You can also set quotas with commission rate accelerators for business developed in target markets. Or, you can simply place a bonus on deals that meet defined criteria in the targeted markets.

2 – Enable Your Sales Team to Realize Their Personal and Professional Goals

On the flip side of the company goals are the rep's personal and professional goals – what's in it for the sales representative. You should design your sales compensation plan to keep your sales reps motivated and engaged. In this section, let's review the primary drivers for sales representative motivation:

- Satisfaction of having professional expertise

- Realistic earnings expectations

- An opportunity to share in significant earnings upside if they exceed their goals

- Money as a measure of success

- The esteem of their family and peers

- The flexibility to enjoy their earnings

Satisfaction of Having Professional Expertise

Sales representatives want and need to feel that they are experts in their field. Providing your sales team with proper sales, industry and product training will develop their expertise and go a long way toward keeping them professionally satisfied. Maintaining professional expertise is an important area for training. For more on this topic, see Element 5: Develop and Manage Your People, Chapter 14: Training.

Realistic Earnings Expectations

From the sales representatives' perspective, sales compensation plans must demonstrate realistic earnings potential. The sales reps must be able to see a path to earning the compensation they target for themselves. For earnings expectations to be realistic, the goals or quotas set for the rep must be attainable. If the quotas are set too high, the sales reps will discount their ability to surpass the target and not work as hard as they might otherwise work to reach the goal. Similarly, if the commission payout rate (i.e., the amount of commissions paid on each dollar of revenue generated) is too low, the reps will view themselves as underpaid and will likely look for new jobs.

A best practice is to show your sales representatives how much they can earn given various scenarios:

- If they fail to reach their targets

- If they meet quota at 100%

- If they significantly surpass their quota

If possible, build an earnings model in Excel or an online web app so that the sales reps can test their own sales scenarios to see how much they would earn.

Share in Earnings Upside

Sales representatives are competitive; they like to be recognized when they exceed expectations. Sales representatives will drive harder when they share in the upside of a highly profitable deal or significantly exceed quota.

Money as a Measure of Success

Sales representatives certainly value money and cash compensation. And sales reps will often use money as a measure of their professional success. In the overall picture, reps earning $300,000 will hold themselves in higher regard than those earning $200,000. If you challenge these same two sales reps in a contest where the winner receives $500 and the runner up receives $250, the esteem of the winner of the $500 award will rise considerably in the eyes of peers.

While money may not be the only motivator for sales reps, they do use it to keep score.

Esteem of Family and Peers

Successful sales representatives are competitive by nature. They like recognition and they like to know they are valuable to the organization, their family and their peers. Given this, I've found it useful to build non-commission compensation into the sales compensation plan.

These forms of recognition can be as simple as a certificate, plaque or trophy presented at an all-company meeting or a special parking space for the "rep of the month." Sales reps love to be recognized before their peers. Other forms of compensation may include winning a desk with a window view, a company car, or an award trip for top performers. Award trips can be especially motivating when spouses or other family members are included.

Flexibility to Enjoy Earnings

As sales representatives attain greater success, cash compensation gains a partner in flexibility to enjoy those earnings. Sales representatives will look to convert their earnings into other tangible assets to demonstrate their success. These may be a larger house, a nicer car, a boat, vacations or jewelry. Whatever it is, with success, sales representatives need to be able to enjoy the fruits of their success to stay engaged. Give your successful sales reps time to re-energize and enjoy what they've earned.

3 – Attract and Retain Top Sales Representatives

The third purpose of your sales compensation plan is to attract and retain good sales representatives. A well-designed sales compensation plan helps retain good sales representatives by:

- Providing rewards for results and excellence

- Bolstering the self-esteem of top performers

- Offering a pathway to achieving personal and professional goals, which will also help you attract other top performers from within your industry.

The advantage of attracting and retaining top sales representatives is a reduced level of required sales investment. When you retain your best sales reps and attract top talent in your industry, your training costs are reduced since your reps already have proven sales skills. Training is still necessary for products and company culture, but sales skills training is likely to involve only regular refreshers rather than wholesale training from the ground up.

Additionally, your sales cycle is also likely to be faster because talented, established sales representatives who already have strong market knowledge and awareness, as well as existing customer relationships, can produce results faster. With respect to developing new business, established business development representatives are skilled in lead generation, nurturing and closing, so the cost there will be lower as well.

Characteristics of a Well-Designed Compensation Plan

A well-designed sales compensation plan has the following characteristics:

- **The plan reinforces the business goals and strategy.** Earnings are tied to and reinforce the business goals and strategy. This is true whether the goals are revenue, market share, products, targeted customers, business development, customer satisfaction or anything else.

- **The plan is easy to understand.** Strive to have only 2 to 3 payout components in your plan. This requires you to be laser-focused so that your sales representatives understand where you want them to spend their time and resources. An easily understood plan also motivates your sales reps more effectively since they can readily see how they can make money.

- **The plan is easy to administer.** Plans should be easy to administer so that you can pay your sales reps promptly when commissions are due. Without an easily administered plan, you may need to divert important finance department resources to paying commissions so that you pay on time. If, because of plan complexity, you make errors in commission payments, your sales reps will begin keeping their own commission tallies to double check your payouts. This results in sales reps wasting time tracking commissions rather than selling.

- **The plan is differentiated to motivate each functional role in the sales organization.** In other words, it's okay to have different sales compensation plans for different roles and different types of sales reps. Field sales reps are fundamentally different from inside sales reps and they have different goals. Therefore, they should have different compensation plans. Similarly, account managers are different from business development reps and lead generation specialists differ from closers. Pay each salesperson so that you drive the desired behavior and reward the desired results for their roles.

Let's look at the basic components of a sales compensation plan:

- Base salary

- Draw

- Variable compensation

- Terms and conditions

Base Salary

Base salary is paid for the timely and accurate completion of administrative and other tasks associated with the generation of sales volumes, including:

- Managing account relationships

- Prospecting for new business

- Ensuring profitability of deals

- Competitive reporting

- Forecasting business volumes

- Negotiating master agreements

- Assisting in the collection of accounts receivable

- Expense reporting

- Personal education/skill development

- Completion of all required documentation

Draw

To supplement base salary, a draw is a loan your company provides to each sales representative that they repay through earned commissions. Draw amounts are usually negotiated with sales representatives for a defined start-up period when they are hired. The draw is designed to provide the sales representatives with nominal cash flow while they are focused on developing the territory. For businesses with seasonal cycles, draws can also be used to provide reps with more predictable cash flow.

Draws can be either recoverable or non-recoverable. Recoverable draws are loans the company makes against future commissions or bonuses. Each month during the draw period, you pay your sales rep the draw amount. If your sales rep earns commissions that are less than the draw amount, you pay your rep the commissions plus enough draw so that the commissions plus the draw total the amount of the full draw. The outstanding draw amount accumulates from month to month. When earned commissions exceed the draw, you use the excess commissions to repay the outstanding draw. Once the accumulated draw is repaid, all commissions are paid directly to the sales representative.

Non-recoverable draws are also loans against future commissions or bonuses. However, a non-recoverable draw guarantees your sales representative a minimum level of income for each commission period. If earned commissions are less than the draw amount, your sales rep still receives the draw amount. No accumulated draw is carried into the next commission period.

Variable Compensation

The variable compensation portion of your sales compensation plan can be made up of three components:

- **Commissions** are earnings tied to sales revenue. The more sales revenue your sales representative generates, the more commissions the sales representative earns.

- **Bonuses** are earnings tied to pre-defined goals. You may pay bonuses for surpassing quota, achieving target product levels or surpassing the company's profitability threshold.

- **Performance awards** are payments designed to reward superior performance, recognize contributions to achieving business milestones or otherwise compensate your sales reps for positive activities not otherwise recognized by commissions or bonuses.

Your business's goals such as revenue, margin and product volume are usually assigned to sales representatives in the form of quotas. Quotas become the basis for measuring performance and paying commissions, bonuses and awards.

See Appendix V – Sample Commission Schedule for an example of a simple variable commission plan.

Terms and Conditions

Finally, terms and conditions provide your senior management with the tools it needs to administer the sales compensation plan while protecting your company's interests. Let's look at some of the key terms and conditions that I always include when writing a sales compensation plan.

Commission Earned

This defines the point at which you recognize that commissions are earned. It occurs between when the sales reps complete their work and when your company is assured the sale will close and revenue will be collected. Trigger points can be:

- Receipt of purchase order

- Installation or delivery of product

- Invoice to customer

- Receipt of payment from customer

Commission Paid

Commissions are paid days or weeks after the commissions are earned. This time lag allows your company to prepare commission statements and checks on a regular cycle. It also offers additional confidence that customers will not cancel the sales on which commissions are paid. Commission payment cycles usually fall at the end of the month or quarter in which the commissions are earned, or sometimes in the month or quarter immediately following the period in which commissions are earned. Some companies pay commissions within a defined number of days of commissions being earned. I recommend keeping to a regular schedule tied to normal payroll periods.

Recovery of Payments

Sometimes customers will rescind a sale after commissions are paid. Or by mistake you may overpay or make incorrect payments. For these situations, you need to include a clause that allows your company to recover overpayments. This term may also be used to define recovery of draws or payments resulting from misrepresentation by the sales rep.

Disputes

Disputes can arise from disagreements on the amount of commissions paid, when commissions are earned, how commissions are shared with other sales reps or whether a customer falls within or outside a sales rep's territory. Who's the final arbiter of disputes? I recommend designating your sales leader or the president of the company or business unit to make the final call.

Shared Commission Credit

As with disputes, the sales leader should decide when commissions should be shared among contributing sales representatives. These situations arise when a sale is spread across multiple territories or when more than one sales rep makes key contributions to closing the sale.

Windfall Business

On occasion, business comes in without any work or contribution by the assigned sales representative, based solely on the company's reputation. In the case of true "windfall business," your company should reserve the right to pay all, partial or no commission.

Misrepresentations

Your company should reserve the right to deny commissions on any business that results from misrepresentation on the part of the sales representative or the customer.

Acceptance of Transactions

Your company should also reserve the right to accept or reject any transaction brought to it by the sales representative. You decide what is acceptable business, not the sales representative.

Partial Year Participants

Over the course of a year, you will hire new sales reps, fire reps, have reps resign or retire and reassign sales reps to new territories or new responsibilities. Your plan should address how commissions are handled in these situations. Try using these terms:

- ***New sales reps*** will be paid commissions on business they close and for which they made a direct contribution.

- ***Sales reps assigned to a new territory*** will be paid full commission on business they closed in their old territory. Full commissions will be paid on business they initiate and close in their new territory. Split commission or partial commission (according to value of their contribution) will be paid on all other business in old and new territories.

- ***Sales reps assigned to new responsibilities (non-territory sales)*** will be paid full commission on business they closed in their old territory. Split commission or partial commission (according to value of their contribution) will be paid on all other business in the old territory.

- ***Sales reps who retire*** will be paid full commission on business they closed in their old territory. Split commission or partial commission (according to value of their contribution) will be paid on all other business in the old territory.

- ***Sales reps who resign or are fired*** forfeit unpaid commissions and commission credits upon leaving employment of the company. (Be sure to review this clause with your company's employment attorney to ensure that it conforms to applicable laws.)

Changing of Plan

To allow your company to adjust to changing market conditions, include a clause that allows you to change or amend the sales compensation plan at any time.

Interpretation of Plan

Situations will arise that do not fit neatly into the sales compensation plan as it was envisioned or written. Include a clause that defines who will interpret the plan in these situations. I recommend assigning interpretation of the plan to the sales leader.

These terms and conditions should cover most situations. However, you may want to include additional terms that your company may need to address its specific needs and control its business. Overall, you need to present a balanced and reasonably fair document to your sales team. If the sales plan has too many administrative terms and heavily favors the company, it may kill sales rep motivation. However, a sales plan with too few terms may leave the company exposed to reps who take advantage of every loophole and opportunity.

As you build your sales team, tie your compensation, bonuses and awards to specific goals and actions that will support achieving the company's strategic goals. This is what drives specific performance.

Chapter 18: Accountability

"Successful teams are built on accountability."

In Element 1: Establish Your Foundation, we discussed how to set goals and build a strategic plan. We also discussed the importance of defining metrics to measure team or sales rep progress toward their goals. This element deals with holding sales reps accountable to their commitments and reviewing performance against agreed-on business and territory plans.

Accountable to Commitments

A key tenet of management is holding your sales team accountable for the commitments they make to you, their company, their teammates and their customers. Commitments can range from accepting a sales quota in return for receiving a territory to work in to making the number of sales calls needed each day or week to uncover opportunities or develop prospects. With customers, commitments may be honesty in explaining features and benefits, promises of availability and delivery schedules, and performance guarantees.

If sales reps fail to honor their commitments, then it is the manager's responsibility to hold the sales reps accountable. Sales managers can use a range of tactics to hold sales reps accountable. A timely quiet conversation can often remind sales reps of their commitments and your expectation that they will deliver on those commitments. If a quiet conversation is not sufficient to change your rep's behavior, then you can escalate to a formal meeting where you review the commitments that the rep has made and discuss the rep's failure to meet the commitments. This discussion may include a plan of actions that the sales rep must take to ensure the rep meets commitments.

If your sales rep continues to fail to meet commitments, then you may consider putting the sales rep on a performance improvement plan (PIP). Details on PIPs and how they work are covered in Chapter 15: Performance Management.

Review and Adapt Your Plans

Not all forms of accountability result from a failure to meet commitments. Strategic plan reviews and territory plan reviews are accountability tools that you should use proactively. Plan reviews help to ensure that your sales team is on track to meet their goals and commitments throughout the year, before there is a problem.

As a sales leader, you should review your plans regularly. There are two plans you must review: the strategic plan, also referred to as the business plan, and the sales plan, which is commonly referred to as the territory plan. I recommend conducting reviews at least once a quarter. Bimonthly is better if you are selling into a market that changes rapidly or has a sales cycle of fewer than four weeks.

Strategic Plan Review

The purpose of the strategic plan review is fourfold:

1. Assess the assumptions that underpin the plan

2. Determine if the assumptions continue to be valid

3. Identify changes in the market that have affected or will affect the validity of the assumptions

4. Adjust the plan to reflect market changes so that the company continues on a path to realize its goals

Your plan review may determine that market conditions have changed to a degree that achievement of certain strategic goals is no longer viable, or that the original assumptions were faulty or invalid and cannot be fixed. To address this, the sales leader must work with the company's executive team to reassess the company's goals and develop a new plan accordingly.

Within the strategic plan, I recommend reviewing products, key customers, targeted new customers and targeted markets. Also, review company goals, metrics designed to assess progress toward achieving those goals, commitments to short-term targets between now and the next scheduled plan review, status of previous short-term commitments and other leading indicators of success or failure. In Appendix VI – Strategic Plan Review – Questions to Ask, I have included some questions you should cover in your strategic plan review.

Sales Plan Review

The sales plan review covers all the points covered in the strategic plan review but covers them at a territory level. Here's a summary of what you should review for each territory:

- Gross profit attainment versus quota and plan

- Selling plan for balance of quarter/year:
    - New opportunities
    - Existing opportunities
    - Account penetration
    - Product expansion
    - Actions needed to fulfill plan

- Changes in accounts:
    - Contacts, executives
    - Strategies
    - Merger and acquisition activities
    - Regulatory
    - Competitive

- Other progress in the territory (not covered above)

Competitive Reviews and Opportunity Loss Reviews

It's important to review two specific areas that have a major effect on the overall sales plan: competition and lost opportunities. Competitive reviews should be conducted when targeting competitive sales opportunities, introducing new products or entering new markets. Opportunity loss reviews should be conducted whenever key sales opportunities are lost either to competitors or when the customer decides not to move forward with a purchase at all.

- **Competitive reviews** – Review of market competition trends and how they affect your sales efforts. I recommend holding competitive reviews at least annually, but also whenever there is a substantial change in the competitive landscape. Cover these areas in your competitive review:
  - Key competitors
    - Names of dominant competitors
    - Market share – Size of competitor and percent market share
    - Product and service offerings – Including features and pricing
    - Differentiators – Strengths and weaknesses
    - How you compete against them
  - Positioning – How your company and its products are positioned in the market vs. competitors
    - Needs being met
    - Key features and benefits
    - Competitive advantages
    - Competitive weaknesses

- **Opportunity loss reviews** – Conduct these reviews following any significant opportunity loss. A significant opportunity loss is defined as an opportunity lost to a competitor (most likely) or to no action on the part of the customer. The opportunity should be significant to the company if it represents:

  o A failure to gain a foothold or penetration in a target market or target prospect account

  o A loss that enabled a competitor to gain entry to a key account

  o A loss of significant revenue size that your company had a reasonable expectation of winning

  The purpose of the loss review is to evaluate the circumstances of the loss including:

  o What could have been done differently to prevent the loss?

  o What were the factors that contributed to the loss?

    - Price – Was our solution price competitive, including total cost of ownership (warranty, maintenance, support)?

    - Product availability – Could we deliver the product when the customer needed it and at a time equal to or better than our competitors?

    - Company capability – Did the customer have confidence in our ability to perform to the level needed?

    - Product features – Did our product or solution have all the features needed to solve the customer's problem?

- Customer or executive relationships – Was our sales team selling to the right contacts at the customer? Does the customer know and trust us?

o Who was the competition and how did we fare against them?

Element 7: Coordinate With the Rest of Your Business

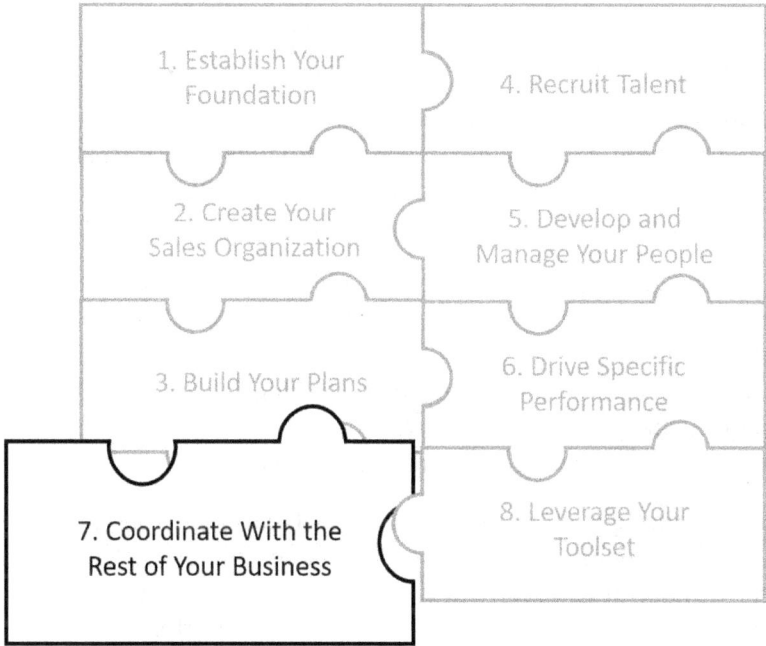

"No one can whistle a symphony.
It takes a whole orchestra to play it."

—*H.E. Luccock, Yale Divinity School*

Sales is the engine that drives a company. Without sales, there is no need for the other functions of a company. Finance has no capital to track. Marketing has no leads to generate. Operations has nothing to produce. Human resources has no people to recruit and develop.

One may argue that without sales the company has no reason for being — there are no customers, no products to make for customers and no money to pay for the products or anything else in the company.

Without sales, a company eventually runs down its cash and resources and goes out of business.

When sales coordinates with the other functional areas of the company, finance, operations, research and development and human resources, the result can be a stronger business attuned to the market and poised for growth.

The goods and services a company sells are the basis of the company's value. The revenue that sales generates provides the capital to develop, manufacture and deliver the goods and services. It attracts the capital investors provide to fund the company.

When investors assess whether to put their capital to work in a company, the first thing they look at is the revenue stream. How much revenue is the company generating? When will this revenue convert to cash in the coming years? Sales forecasts identify how much revenue a company expects to generate, when they expect it and from which sources. Sales forecasts project the future health of the company.

Too often, though, sales representatives treat sales forecasting as an exercise done either to make their manager happy or to predict the future with about as much confidence as if they were telling fortunes. It should not be either of these and we now have better tools to forecast sales with greater accuracy than we did even five years ago.

In Chapter 19: Forecasting and Management Meetings, we explore the importance of working with the other functional areas of your business.

Element 7: Coordinate With the Rest of Your Business

PECO*

PECO is a private-equity firm that invests in small- to medium-sized growth businesses. They buy controlling stakes in the companies and introduce operational efficiencies and strategic focus to improve both revenue and profitability. When PECO buys a company, their preference is to leave the management team in place and provide them with guidance and resources they had not previously had access to.

An important tool in PECO's success formula is transparency of information and sharing of information in weekly senior management meetings. In these meetings, each functional leader (CEO, finance, operations, human resources, sales, marketing, information technology, etc.) presents results from the previous week, plans and goals for the coming week, status of work in progress and current challenges or help needed.

By sharing this information with the entire leadership team, the company can focus the power of everyone's experience and perspective to solve problems. They also keep everyone informed of the status of all key performance indicators that measure the company's progress toward its strategic goals. The result is there are few situations, good or bad, that the management team does not anticipate and address early in a cycle.

By communicating and coordinating with the rest of their business, PECO's portfolio companies run smoothly and without surprises.

*Company and individual names have been changed.

Chapter 19: Forecasting and Management Meetings

"The goal is to turn data into information
and information into insight."

— Carly Fiorina, CEO, Hewlett-Packard (1999-2005)

Why Forecasting Is Important

The figure below shows some of the different business areas that make decisions based on sales forecasts. Let's look at each of them in turn.

Finance

The finance department is often the first group you think of when developing sales forecasts. Usually, it's the finance department that is asking for the forecast. Many sales reps view finance as just being full of "bean counters" who need to track everything. Reps often ask why do they need to know what we're going to sell before we even sell it? The answer is simple. Finance needs to make sure the company has the money it needs to operate and grow.

First and foremost, the finance department needs to make sure the company has enough cash on hand to pay its bills – payroll, vendors, suppliers, taxes, loan interest and principal – the list goes on and on. Without enough cash to pay its bills, the organizations that are owed money may force the company into bankruptcy or to close altogether. Cash is the first concern for a viable company. Sales forecasts and projections are vital to letting the finance department know how much cash will be coming into the company and when.

Second, the finance department's next concern is satisfying the company's lenders. As part of a loan agreement, lenders set covenants to which the company must adhere. These covenants often define how much debt the company can assume and how much cash and/or profitability the company must maintain for each quarter. These covenants must be met for the loan to comply with the lender's requirements and for the company to not be in default on the loan. If the covenants are not met, then the lender may place the loan in default and call for the company to repay the balance of the loan immediately. Unless the company has alternate lenders ready to take the original lender's place, then the company would become at risk for not having enough cash to meet its obligations and the company would have to close. So, next to cash availability, loan compliance is next most important to a company's survivability.

Third, finance establishes the company's financial position in terms of its:

- **Balance sheet** – Where the company stands today with respect to assets, liabilities and equity

- **Profit and loss statement** – Whether the company is profitable over a defined period

- **Cash flow** – How much cash the company is generating and how it's using cash

Using these financial statements, finance generally looks back over the last one, three and five years, and then projects forward (based on assumptions of what the company will do) over the next one, three and five years. Sales forecasts are especially important here because the company's forward projections are based on the revenue forecast by sales and the resources needed to meet the sales forecasts.

Once the finance department has settled on its financial projections, which is likely an iterative process, it works with the various departments across the company to set budgets. Budgets include both revenue budgets (in sales, these are called quotas) and expense budgets. These budgets are influenced in large part by your sales targets and forecasts. It's important for the finance department to understand and have visibility into what sales expects to sell and when – in the coming weeks, months and even years.

Operations

It's important for the sales leader to work closely with operations and production. To drive sales and repeat sales, operations needs to deliver the products customers want, when the customers want them. The sales team needs to provide operations with the information they need to produce the goods and maintain sufficient inventories of finished goods.

A company's operations team relies on sales forecasts to determine its production levels, inventory needs and plant utilization. All three are closely tied to each other. Production must deliver enough finished goods in the right product mix to meet customer orders. This means they must have visibility into what sales expects to sell and when. To produce the needed products, operations must have enough raw materials and parts in inventory to build them. This means ordering from suppliers with enough lead time to meet the production demand when it's needed. The sales forecasts also drive plant utilization as operations determines whether to add production lines or shut them down, whether to add a second or third shift to existing lines, and whether to outsource production or build new factories. All these decisions are driven, in large part, by the sales forecasts.

Supply Chain

Your supply chain and logistics department relies heavily on accurate sales forecasts to determine how much materials inventory it needs to maintain and purchase to meet production demands. This, in turn, drives warehouse requirements as well as the logistics involved with moving raw materials and finished goods. How many trucks will the company need? Where will they be needed and when?

In addition, a solid sales forecast and the purchases associated with it drive stronger supplier relationships with associated commitments between the two companies.

Human Resources

Sales forecasts also drive human resource decisions including headcount requirements for departments across the company and hiring plans to meet the headcount needs. These, in turn, determine recruiting needs or plans to reduce the labor force in the company.

In addition to these departments relying on the sales forecasts for their decision making, other groups in the company also make decisions based on what the sales team learns in the market. Product managers need to know: What are customers saying about our products? What features are valued and which are not? What products and features will be needed in the future? How should the company adapt its product line to meet customer expectations and market needs?

The marketing team needs to know what marketing efforts are working. They look for feedback from the sales team to augment the data they monitor and measure for every campaign. Customer service needs to share what they are learning from users and customers so that sales can adjust its sales efforts, presentations and messages. Field service interacts with sales to better understand customer expectations and provide information on product reliability and performance.

Management Meetings

I have found that an excellent way to communicate with counterparts across the company is the most straightforward: hold weekly one-hour management meetings. Structure these meetings for efficiency.

I recommend holding the management meeting every Monday morning at 8 am. Only the department heads who report directly to the company president should attend. The president kicks off the meeting with a 5-minute report identifying important developments from the past week. Then, the department heads get 4 to 5 minutes each to present the status of their department. This meeting can be virtual if some attendees join via videoconference/internet.

Each department presents a single information slide (see Appendix VII - Management Meetings Slide), formatted into four blocks and summarizing the following information:

- **Strategic Progress** – What strategic progress has your department made in the last week?

    o Goals – Status of progress against the department's most important goals

    o Key performance indicators (KPIs) – Progress as measured by the department's KPIs

    o Key initiatives – Status of department's key initiatives (i.e., product introduction or targeted market penetration)

- **Top Tactical Commitments (next 4 weeks)** – What are your department's top commitments for the coming month? These are action statements of what will be done.

    o This week – What was done last week? What will be done this coming week? What commitments were missed?

    o This month – What is your department committed to doing this month?

- **Top Challenges, Caution Flags and Help Needed**

    o Where does your department need help?

    o What are you concerned about that may be an obstacle to your success?

- **People, Leadership and Development**

    o Recognition – Who has done an outstanding job in the last week?

- o Training and development – What training or other professional development is scheduled/needed?

- o Other

Every speaker needs to be prepared and concise. The purpose of the meeting is to share high-level information. Department heads may follow up with their peers after the meeting to learn more, share additional information or help address challenges and solve problems. Communication is key to successful coordination with the rest of the business.

Element 8: Leverage Your Toolset

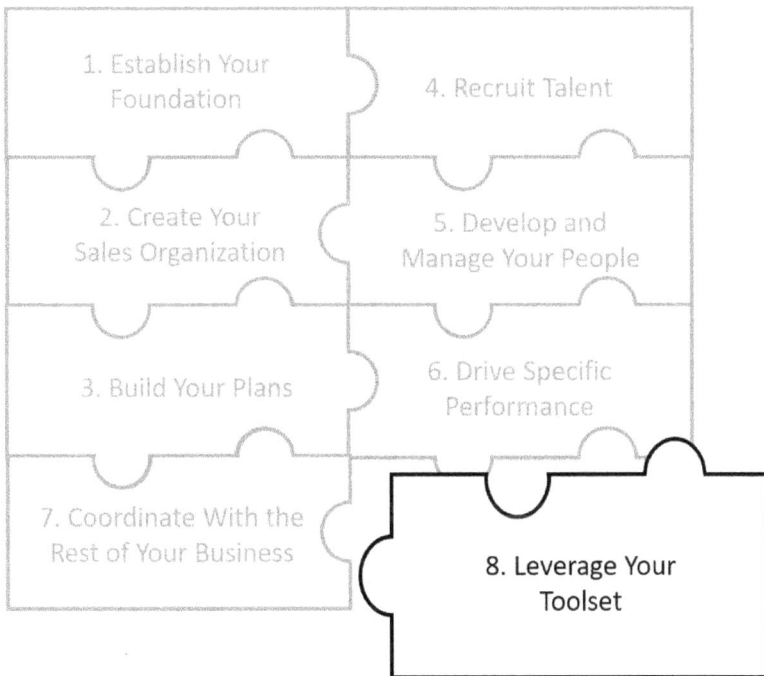

1. Establish Your Foundation
2. Create Your Sales Organization
3. Build Your Plans
4. Recruit Talent
5. Develop and Manage Your People
6. Drive Specific Performance
7. Coordinate With the Rest of Your Business
8. Leverage Your Toolset

"You cannot mandate productivity;
you must provide the tools to let people become their best."

— *Steve Jobs, Apple co-founder*

You've invested in strategy, planning and people. You've implemented training programs and measure performance. Your entire company is set up to work together to achieve the company's goals.

Congratulations! But it could all be for naught if your sales team doesn't have the tools they need to do their jobs.

A wide variety of tools is available to help your team be more effective and more efficient, with ever more tools being developed every day.

Having a well-designed CRM is the most important tool (see Chapter 20: CRM). Other tools help sales reps maximize their productivity and the time they spend with customers (see Chapter 21: Other Important Tools).

Element 8: Leverage Your Toolset

Midwest Logistics*

Midwest Logistics was growing rapidly. They had identified a way to arrange their customers' shipments which allowed them to ship full truckloads of goods with every trip. By maintaining their own warehouses, they could manage customer inventory and retailer demand. They combined this with their own fleet of long-haul tractor trailers so they could always ensure full trucks were going to centralized distribution centers.

Despite efficient operations, Midwest Logistics had trouble keeping track of all their prospects and opportunities. All sales opportunities went through the VP of sales. He saved the most important deals for himself to close and parsed out the rest to his sales team. When the VP of sales moved on to another company, Midwest Logistics found they had a problem.

Their CRM system was not tracking all the information they needed to track. Further, the CRM did not integrate with the company's financial or operations systems. Opportunities were misplaced and data was inconsistent.

Midwest Logistics spent about six months assessing their needs and then selecting and installing a CRM that worked best for them. The IT team customized the CRM to fit their sales process and trained the sales team to use it.

Since installing their CRM, Midwest Logistics has been able to track and manage more business opportunities, close more business and drive more profitable revenue without increasing the size of their sales team. When you leverage your toolset, it pays off.

*Company and individual names have been changed.

Chapter 20: CRM

"The purpose of business is to create and keep a customer."

– Peter Drucker, management guru,
consultant, educator, author

Your customer relationship management system (CRM) may be one of your most critical tools. It enforces discipline on your sales team, provides a central repository for all customer-related information and provides you with the information you need to do effective business planning and reviews.

There are many CRM systems available on the market. They range from all-inclusive, complex systems from vendors such as Salesforce that command premium prices for a premium product to simple, easy-to-use systems that charge little or nothing per user monthly. Define your criteria before selecting a CRM system. Once you select and customize your CRM, it's likely to be the platform you rely on for years to come.

Why Invest in a CRM?

There are many reasons to invest in a CRM — tracking of sales activity, discipline of follow-up and consistency of message and communication. But I think the most valuable reason to invest in a CRM is to gain the power and control it provides through information. A CRM system, implemented and used correctly, provides your sales reps, managers and business leaders with a wealth of information.

- **Sales reps** – Your sales reps benefit from the CRM's wealth of customer information. Everything from a business and industry overview to key contact information to leads and opportunities and even personal information about contacts can be kept in CRM records. Having this information available at any time enables your sales reps to prepare for sales calls efficiently. By using the CRM, reps can know exactly who to speak with, when to speak with them and what to talk about.

The CRM enables them to nurture leads, track opportunities and move deals through the sales cycle. In short, rather than following a "hit or miss" call strategy to find business, your sales reps can use the data in the CRM to target prospects and call customers when the opportunities are ripe for harvest.

- **Sales management** – Your sales management benefits from the CRM's wealth of opportunity and activity information. In the CRM, your managers can view all identified opportunities and see where they stand in the sales cycle and over time. Based on this information, sales management can forecast sales for the coming weeks or months, estimate customer value and determine where to put resources. For example, if a sales manager reviews their sales pipeline from the CRM, the manager might see that over the next six months they have $5 million in potential sales spread evenly across the months. However, if some of the sales scheduled to close in months 2 and 3 have lower likelihoods of closing, the sales manager may decide to reduce forecasted revenue. Or the sales manager may decide to put additional sales support resources on the lower likelihood accounts with the expectation that those deals will be more likely to close if given more attention.

  Sales managers may also use CRM data to coach and direct their sales reps. As sales reps enter their sales activities in the CRM, their sales manager can review the activities and coach them. Are they spending enough time calling? Are they conducting enough face-to-face sales calls? Are they uncovering enough leads or generating enough proposals? Or, are they sending out too many unsolicited proposals? CRM data can help distinguish the efficient sales reps from those who need additional training.

- **Business leaders** – Finally, the business leadership team benefits from a good CRM system by getting views into markets, customers and products. Unlike enterprise resource planning (ERP) systems that provide views of the business based on past transactions, CRM systems provide views into both historical transactions (what has happened) and future transactions (what is expected to happen and when).

On the historical side, your CRM system tracks all transactions that have occurred, including those won, lost, no decision and still open. Further, it can track competitive activity, product mix, time to close and a whole host of data that allows you to assess the effectiveness of your sales force, your marketing campaigns, demand for your products, product mix, competitive activity and more.

On the forward-looking side, your CRM system tracks all leads and opportunities. Based on this information, business leaders have a view into likely sales in the short term and medium term, industry and product trends, and market demand. This information is used for business planning and determining resource requirements for sales, support and service personnel; manufacturing plant requirements; inventory buys; and expected cash or investment needs.

Other Benefits of a CRM System

The primary additional benefit of a CRM system is that it enforces discipline on your sales team. By entering call and lead information in the CRM, sales reps can schedule follow-up calls according to pre-defined time frames based on sales call cycles, sales best practices and company experience. The CRM can automate much of the sales and marketing activities and communications. This results in better lead and opportunity management.

Additionally, your sales team can maintain communication templates within the CRM to ensure calls, emails, letters, proposals, contracts and other communications are consistent, meet your company's standards and present the correct message.

Your CRM also becomes an information repository for collecting data on everything your sales team needs to sell effectively and everything you need to manage your business. Information you should maintain in the CRM includes account history, contact information, account plans and sales collateral, not to mention all customer interactions with your company.

Finally, your CRM facilitates the entire business planning and review process. The CRM makes it easier to access sales pipeline information, conduct sales forecasting and determine win/loss rates.

How to Select a CRM System

First, map out your sales processes:

- How does your sales team sell?
    - Inside sales vs. field sales
    - Inbound leads vs. outbound calling
    - Prospecting vs. account management
    - Commodity vs. complex solution
    - Broad market vs. niche market
- What information do you need to track and what other information should you track?
    - Contact information
    - Range of contacts – Line of business, procurement, executive suite, others
    - Company demographics – Industry, size, locations
    - Company overview – Products, markets
    - Product/plant/office/other specifications
    - Call and contact history – Inbound, outbound, marketing

- What would help your sales reps sell more efficiently?

    o Territory focus – Geographic, industry, markets

    o Sales enablement tools – Spec sheets, proposal generation, call scripts, etc.

    o Availability of information

    o Technology – Laptops, phones, tablets, databases, applications, etc.

Second, define your priorities with respect to what you want to accomplish with your CRM:

- Opportunity tracking

- Sales pipeline management

- Customer follow-up and management

- Information tracking and management

- Sales team management

- Integration with enterprise resource planning (ERP), financial or accounting systems

- Other priorities

Third, research the CRM market to understand the relative strengths of the various offerings. Ask these questions:

- How easy or difficult is the system to implement and use?

- Can I customize the CRM to work well in my environment?

- Will the CRM system allow me to accomplish what I want to do?

- What is the cost of the CRM system?
  - Acquisition, including hardware and software upgrades
  - Implementation and integration
  - User training
  - Monthly user fees
  - Ongoing IT maintenance and service

Finally, map your needs to each CRM system you're considering and select the one that best suits your company. A caution here is to pay specific attention to how well you can build the CRM to work within your environment by fitting the CRM to complement your processes. I recommend that you do not implement the CRM as it comes out of the box and attempt to change your sales processes to fit the CRM. This is a recipe for failure as your sales team will likely continue to follow their "tried and true" methods of selling rather that make the change to using the CRM. Any money you save by not customizing and integrating the CRM will be spent many times over as your sales reps create workarounds to avoid using the CRM.

Chapter 21: Other Important Tools

"The best investment is in the tools of one's own trade."

— Benjamin Franklin, scientist, philosopher,
revolutionary, patriot

As technology continues its inexorable progress, new and better sales management tools become available almost daily. These tools range from social media to collaboration platforms, from cloud-based storage and application servers to mobile sales applications. Plus, time-tested tools such as proposal templates and call scripts continue to be useful. Let's look at some tools available to the sales leader today.

Social Media Tools

Social media tools are important for communications by both sales and marketing.

- **Email** – Email can be used for both one-on-one sales communications and one-on-many communications to a broad audience. In one-on-one communications, sales representatives use email to generate interest, initiate conversations, provide detailed information and deliver proposals, among other reasons. One-on-many communications, or email blasts, are used to announce new information such as product or service offerings, promotions, new offices opening, acquisitions or other information to support the brand or that may be interesting to a large audience or market.

- **Twitter** – Twitter is used for communicating general information to an audience of self-selected followers. Sales and marketing teams may tweet links to blogs, product pages, news articles, white papers and any other online information that supports the brand.

- **LinkedIn** – Companies use LinkedIn as a secondary online home page. It provides a site to deliver a high-level description of your company as well as post articles about products, company announcements and industry news. LinkedIn also provides your company the ability to recruit through job listings. Sales reps use LinkedIn to present themselves and their credentials for customers and prospects to review. More importantly, though, savvy sales reps use LinkedIn as a prospecting tool to find and target potential customers, identify executives and decision makers, and identify routes to getting introductions to new companies or to influencers and decision makers at target companies.

- **Facebook** – Facebook is generally a person-to-person application. However, many businesses use Facebook pages and ads to communicate their message, especially if they have consumer-oriented products.

- **Instagram** – Businesses use Instagram to communicate visual information about their products to users who have elected to follow them. Instagram is like Twitter, but it's based on using images rather than words and links.

- **Google** – Google is the premier search tool on the internet. A secondary tool is Microsoft's Bing. Most consumers and businesses will learn all they can about a product, vendor or supplier through internet research. Therefore, it's important for your business to be easily found through a Google search. Many businesses find they have a strong return on the investment they make in developing search-friendly websites and implementing search engine optimization (SEO).

- **Others** – There are many other social media tools available to businesses to drive sales and revenue. You should research the tools that have both broad applications to reach a wide audience and niche applications to communicate with the prospects and customers in your industry.

Collaboration Tools

Collaboration tools facilitate teams working together when they are physically distant. The distances may be short or long, but the key is to provide collaboration tools that enable team members to work in the comfort or convenience of their own work area.

Often collaboration meeting tools are used to bring a presentation or product to the office of a customer or prospect without having to incur travel costs. This allows a sales rep to deliver more presentations to more prospects in a smaller window of time.

Some of the more common collaboration meeting tools available are:

- **Microsoft Teams** – Audio and video meetings for up to 250 participants, file sharing, chat and messaging. Teams incorporates and expands on functions available on Skype for Business.

- **Google Meet** – Audio and video meetings (for up to 100 participants with the Enterprise edition), file sharing and messaging.

- **Webex** – Audio and video online meetings and presentations for up to 1,000 participants. Also offers post-meeting file sharing, group messaging and white boarding.

- **GoToMeeting** – Audio and video online conferencing (for up to 3,000 participants with the Enterprise version).

- **Zoom** – Audio and video meetings and presentations with breakout rooms and separate workspaces. Zoom also offers the ability to conduct events with up to 100 live panelists presenting to up to 50,000 participants. Zoom shot to the forefront of collaboration tools with the advent of the 2020 COVID-19 pandemic.

Other collaboration tools can be valuable when team members working remotely need to work together to develop proposals, marketing materials, reports or any other joint project. These tools enable multiple people to work simultaneously on the same file through cloud-based applications. The best-known and most used products are available through Google (Google Workspace) and Microsoft (Office 365).

Cloud-Based File Repositories and Application Servers

Cloud servers are changing how information is shared across teams and with customers. They enable immediate access to information with the ability to define security parameters for individual users or classes of users. Cloud servers allow you to store current and historical files, provide system backups and run applications across a variety of user platforms.

The leading cloud-based services offer a very wide range of sophisticated technology and services that drive development, data storage, applications, security, artificial intelligence, machine learning and much more. Some of the leading cloud-based services include:

- **Amazon Web Services (AWS)** – AWS is currently the leading provider of web services. Its platform drives sales for thousands of companies, large and small.

- **Microsoft Azure** – Azure provides a range of development tools as well as hosting of secure data and applications for a range of businesses.

- **Google Cloud Platform (GCP)** – GCP provides a suite of cloud computing services running on the same infrastructure that runs the applications Google offers to its own end users, such as YouTube and Search.

Sales Apps

There are many sales applications available on the market to simplify the back-office work needed to support your sales team. These include:

- **Commission calculators** – These tools provide the power for sales reps and the management team to calculate payable commissions based on your sales compensation plan and transactions as they are sold. Access to the commission calculator can be local or remote, in office or mobile. Management determines the security settings.

- **Configure, Price, Quote (CPQ)** – CPQ tools simplify, relatively speaking, the process of designing, pricing and quoting complex solutions. They ensure that all prerequisite and co-requisite products and features are included in the solution, thereby reducing the possibility of errors and surprises upon installation.

- **Email tools** – Tools such as Constant Contact and Mailchimp allow your sales reps and marketing team to stay in touch with your customers by delivering regular and timely communications. They keep your team and offering top of mind for prospects in the market for your products and services.

- **DocuSign** – This application enables sales reps and customers to share and sign proposals, contracts and agreements virtually, eliminating the delay associated with obtaining in-person or physical signatures while maintaining the security and veracity of the signatures.

- **Others** – There are hundreds of other applications available. As needs develop, do internet research, network with colleagues and find the ones that will best address your needs.

Templates

Templates are especially useful tools that are too often underused. I've worked with many companies where the sales teams create unique proposals for every customer and every sale. When I asked why, the response was usually that every customer situation was unique and they needed to tailor the proposal to meet each situation or risk losing the deal.

However, I've found that 90% of most company's deals are very much alike, and those differences that do occur are relatively small. By using templates for email communications, presentations, proposals and legal agreements, most companies can realize greater efficiency, deliver more consistent content and generate higher quality products without sacrificing competitiveness or win rates.

When using templates, I recommend that the marketing team and senior sales reps collaborate to create a set of templates that address 80% to 90% of the situations that reps face. Then sales reps should be allowed to customize the templates for each sales situation. Customization may be as minor as inserting the customer name and address, or it may be more involved to include descriptions of the customer's challenges. Product and service descriptions and language can be added or deleted to meet the specific customer's needs.

By using templated deliverables, your reps can meet each customer's needs, provide complete and correct information and present high-quality documents. Plus, the time to create a templated deliverable — an email, presentation, proposal or contract — is considerably shorter than having to create an original deliverable from scratch.

Call Scripts

Call scripts are templates for sales conversations. They can be customized for each call, but they serve as a guide for gathering the information that should be covered in a sales call.

Some sales managers create sales scripts that reps use verbatim. These are often used in outbound sales call centers where the product is simple, even commodity-like, and the sales reps are inexperienced. In sales situations where your sales reps are smart and experienced, where you trust your sales reps to present themselves well and react to fluid customer conversations, and where the product or service may be more complex, you can still use call scripts. But instead of providing a word-for-word script, feature bullet points in the script. Each bullet point can represent an important area to cover at the appropriate point in the sales call. A bulleted script allows the sales rep more flexibility to lead the conversation using natural language questions and cadences.

Element 8: Other Important Tools

The most successful companies equip their sales reps with a set of tools they can use to maximize their productivity and the time they spend with their customers and prospects.

In Closing

"There will be interruptions, and
I don't know when they will occur, and
I don't how deep they will occur;
I do know they will occur from time to time, and
I also know that we'll come out better on the other end."

– Warren Buffet, investor, CEO Berkshire Hathaway

As I was writing *The Sales Executive Handbook*, the world was stricken by the COVID-19 pandemic. This global health crisis shut down whole economies for months at a time. Nearly all businesses, large and small shut their offices. In many instances, plants were idled for weeks and months. Some businesses, particularly small businesses, closed permanently.

Traditional modes of doing business disappeared overnight. Customers did not want sales reps to make in-person sales calls. Trade shows around the world – venues often used to meet customers and identify prospects – were cancelled. Relationships nurtured over time and over meals and entertainment events were placed on hold.

Many companies saw their sales efforts founder and their revenues dry up.

However, the companies that successfully weathered the pandemic adjusted their sales efforts to accommodate the new business environment. Savvy sales executives reviewed their eight essential elements of sales management, made changes where necessary and got back to selling. Some adjusted their plans; others took the time to make changes to their sales team. Many smart sales executives used the slowdown to train their sales reps. All of them engaged their counterparts across their companies to prepare themselves for the inevitable return to production. Finally, as they ramped up again, they employed new sales tools, especially video conferencing and remote demonstration.

As Warren Buffet stated, there will be interruptions. I have found that the most successful sales executives use the eight essential elements of sales management both in the regular course of business but also during ever-increasing disruptions. That's why they come out ahead.

Appendices

I – Sections of the Strategic Plan

A complete strategic plan has eight sections:

- Executive Overview

- Company Description

- Products and Services

- Marketing Plan

- Operations Plan

- Management and Organization

- Financials

- Appendices

Let's look at each section:

- **Executive Overview** – This is a one-page high-level summary of the plan, so that if a person were to read only one part of the plan, it would be the executive overview. After reading the executive overview, the reader (an executive or potential investor/lender) should have a good grasp of your plan.

- **Company Description** – This is a detailed description of your company:

  o What your company does, why you're in business, what your goals are

  o A description of your company's culture

  o The industries you serve and customers you target

    o Why your customers would buy from your company rather than from your competitors (quality, price, availability, delivery, technology, etc.)

    o What your company's legal structure (C-corp, S-corp, Limited Liability Company (LLC), LLP, partnership, sole proprietor, independent contractor) is

- **Products and Services** – This section describes each of the company's key products and services, including the benefit or value that each product or service provides your customers. It also includes any competitive advantages your company's products have over competitors' offerings. It answers these questions:

    o What problems or challenges do the products solve?

    o What are advantages of your products versus those of your competitors?

    o How are the products priced?

    o How are the prices perceived by the market?

    o How do the prices compare with the competition?

- **Marketing Plan** – The marketing plan is the largest and most comprehensive section of the business plan. Here you present all available information about your target market and how your company will penetrate the market. If your company is selling into multiple, distinct markets, then each market should be described, analyzed and evaluated. Include features or characteristics of the market that will affect your business. In addition to the analysis of the target market, your marketing plan should specially address:

    o **Products** – What are the features and benefits? How will you service your customers after making a sale, if at all?

- o **Customers** – What does your ideal customer look like? I recommend developing an "ideal customer profile" that identifies the characteristics of your best customers – not necessarily what you want from customers to make your life easy, but what your actual top customers look like. What do they have in common? What compels them to buy from your company? (See Appendix IV for an ideal customer profile outline.)

- o **Competition** – Who are your key competitors? What makes them successful, especially when competing against your company? Where do your competitors focus their efforts?

- o **Niche** – What is your company's unique competitive niche, the space where your company does best and dominates, or avoids, the competition? A niche is a combination of product, target market and ideal customers.

- o **Strategy** – How will your company compete in your target market? How will your company develop and present its "brand"?

  - ▪ **Promotion** – How do you get the word out, both paid and unpaid? This includes traditional avenues like advertising, trade shows and public relations. It also includes social media such as email campaigns, LinkedIn, Twitter, Facebook, Pinterest, Instagram, YouTube, etc.

  - ▪ **Budget** – How much can your company afford? How much are you willing to pay to build and support your brand?

- **Pricing** – How will your company price its products? Premium pricing? Discount pricing? Pricing to buy or protect market share? Pricing to achieve a target margin? How does your pricing compare with the competition's prices? What is your company's credit policy?

○ **Sales Forecasts** – How much volume and revenue do you expect to sell to your customers? This is very important as it affects other parts of your business, as discussed in Chapter 18: Forecasting and Management Meetings.

- **Production** – How much product does the plant need to produce and when?

- **Purchasing** – How much material needs to be purchased to produce the products and when?

- **Finance** – How much cash is needed to produce the products? When will cash come in from sales to cover your cash needs? How much do you need to borrow?

- **Operations** – How many plant shifts do you need to run to meet production demand? Do you need to build more production capacity or rent it?

- **Human Resources** – Do you need to expand your sales force? How much administrative staff do you need to support operations? Do you need to hire more skilled labor in manufacturing, quality assurance, research and development, etc.?

- **Operations Plan** – What do you need to run the business? What resources do you need to produce your products and services?

  o **Location** – Are there attractive or unattractive locations for production? Warehousing? Shipping? Customer service? Receiving?

  o **Legal structure** – What's the best legal structure for your company? Why?

  o **Personnel** – What roles or positions do you need to fill to produce, sell and manage? What skills are needed? What is the market rate for needed resources?

  o **Production/Sourcing** – Do you buy parts/components or make your own?

  o **Inventory management** – Inventory can be a huge investment of capital. How can you manage it efficiently? How can your suppliers/vendors help you to be more efficient?

  o **Suppliers** – Who are your suppliers? Do they meet your needs? Do you have alternate suppliers in the event a primary supplier cannot meet your needs? What are suppliers' credit terms, so you can manage cash flow?

  o **Credit policies** – What are your company's credit policies? Will you offer discounts for quick payment of invoices? What are your credit terms? How much does it cost your company to extend credit to customers? How many customers would be affected if you tighten/loosen your credit terms? Which customers would be affected? What is your policy on payables?

- **Management and Organization** – This section provides an overview of company management including names of the key executives, an organization chart and the names of outside advisors who influence company decisions.

- **Financials** – The financials section should show the company's health and ability to support its operations while delivering a return to its owners or investors. This section of the business plan should look back for three years and forward for five years in addition to presenting the company's current financial status. There are four important documents in the financials section:

  o **Balance sheet** – This financial statement is a snapshot taken as of a specific date. It shows short-term and long-term assets, short-term and long-term liabilities, and invested equity (both capital put into the company and earnings retained by the company from earlier operations).

  o **Profit and loss statement (P&L)** – This financial statement shows how much money the company made or lost over a period, usually one year, but it can also cover a quarter or month. Key sections of the P&L statement are:

    ▪ **Profit from goods sold (i.e., gross profit):** Revenue minus Variable expenses

    ▪ **Profit from operations before interest, taxes and non-cash expenses (i.e., EBITDA):** Revenue minus Variable expenses and Fixed expenses

    ▪ **Bottom-line profit (i.e., net profit):** EBITDA minus interest, taxes, depreciation and amortization

- o **Cash flow statement** – This statement shows how much cash is available to the company over defined periods of time. Cash flow is important because although a business may be profitable, it may not have enough cash on hand at times to meet its needs (i.e., pay suppliers, meet payroll, etc.). Conversely, a company may not turn a profit, but still be cash rich because of a capital infusion (stock sale, bond sale, bank loan, previous cash surplus).

- o **Sales and revenue forecast** – As mentioned earlier the sales and revenue forecast is an indicator of future cash flows and profitability. More importantly, the sales forecast shows the timing of future cash flow and profitability.

- **Appendices** – The appendices section provides an area where you can include additional, relevant information about your company, market, operations, etc. that did not fit neatly into one of the other sections.

II – Probing Questions for a Territory Review

High-Level Questions

- Is the territory generating results that meet or exceed year-to-date (or quarter-to-date, etc.) targets?
    - If so, what factors have driven success?
        - Sales rep activity levels? Which activities?
        - Market demand for our products? What's driving it?
        - Pricing?
        - Availability?
        - How do we replicate our successes?
    - If not, what are the obstacles that are impeding success?
        - Competition?
        - Product quality?
        - Sales rep activities?
        - What can we do to overcome the obstacles?

Drill-Down Questions

- Are all key accounts performing well against targets?
- Are we selling a preferred mix of products?
- Are the financials meeting or exceeding expectations?
    - Revenue
    - Gross profit
    - Margin percentages

- Where is the sales rep spending time and resources?

- What sales activities are yielding desired results? And where?

- What else can we do to drive better results?

- Are the assumptions and targets for each account/industry/ geography correct?

  - If not, what's changed?

  - What have we learned?

  - How can we apply our lessons learned to other territories?

III – Sample Interview Questions

When interviewing to hire sales professionals, you want to glean as much as you can to determine if they have the skills, ability and desire to excel in the job you are hiring them for. You also need to determine if the candidates will work well within your company's culture. Below are some questions you may want to ask candidates as you conduct interviews.

Sales Leaders (VPs and Managers) *

Business Strategy, Vision, General Management, Track Record

- Tell me about sales organizations you've led in the past. Look for evidence of success:

  o Business outcomes – Year-over-year sales growth, performance versus goals

  o Career progression – Promotions, increased responsibilities

- What experiences have you had with transformation of a sales organization? What was the impact on revenue attainment and overall business performance?

  o Size of company

  o Industries

  o Other facts – Size of organization, areas managed, etc.

- Tell me about your career choices

  o Why did you join each company?

  o Why did you leave each company/position?

  o Pick a company you worked with and tell me why it was a good or bad choice.

Scaling Teams, Culture, Driving Revenue

- Tell me about a time you built or grew a sales team.

  o Tell me about positions you top-graded or replaced.

- o Why was that needed?
- o How did you assess the need?
- Tell me about a time in your career when you transformed an organization from the top down?
  - o What issues did you face?
  - o What strategies and tactics did you employ?
  - o What was the outcome?
- Share some examples of when you helped drive major increases in revenue or improvements in sales effectiveness.
  - o What led to those successes?
- What is your leadership style?
  - o How do you lead and realize target results? Via influence or authority?
  - o Take me through your process.
- How do you allocate/spend time in your role as a sales leader?
  - o Take me through your typical day or week.
  - o What is your role versus the role of your frontline managers?
  - o What do you emphasize and why?
- What reporting metrics do you use?
  - o How did you know when there was an issue?
  - o What did you do when there was an issue?
  - o How do you determine if there is enough opportunity in the pipeline to meet your sales goals?
- What is your overall sales process and methodology? Please take me through it.
  - o How do you get your team to adopt this methodology?

Recruiting Talent

- How do you source sales talent? (Look for how they set candidate profiles, target candidates, screen, engage.)

- Step me through your interview process.

- How do you assess candidates?

- What characteristics do you look for in a candidate?

Organization and Management Experience

- Give me an example of how you identified a low-performing employee and helped them become successful.

- Tell me about an unsuccessful employee you inherited who went on to be successful under your leadership.

  o Why were they successful?

  o What did you have to do to help them achieve success?

*Adapted with permission from a candidate scorecard developed by the executive search firm The Millard Group, www.themillardgroup.com.

Sales Representatives**

Position Fit

- Tell me about yourself.

- Take me through your sales experience so far.

- What do you know about our company?

- How did you prepare for this interview?

- What sales metrics do you track for yourself?

  o How often do you review them?

  o What achievement levels versus your metrics do you consider to be good?

  o What levels do you consider to be excellent?

- Describe a day in your current job.

Sales Skills

- What are your top three open-ended questions for an initial sales call?

- What are the most important skills needed to succeed in sales? How would you rate your skill level in each area?

- Describe a time when your company did not deliver on its product/service to your customer.

  o How did you respond?

- What do you do when a prospect says...?

  o Your price is too high.

  o I need to think it over.

  o We're too busy right now to take on a project like you're recommending.

- How do you qualify your prospects? Take me through your process.
  - What questions do you ask?
  - What signals do you look for that indicate your prospect isn't a good fit?
- What do you see as the key skills in negotiating? How would you rate your skill level in each area?
- How do you close a sales call? Take me through your approach.
- How do you ensure your sales forecasts are accurate?
- How do you build and maintain your sales pipeline?

Competitiveness
- What are your sales goals for this year?
  - Next year?
  - Why not higher?
- Tell me about a deal you closed that you are most proud of.
- How would your colleagues across the company describe you and the work you do?

Work Ethic
- How do you keep your sales skills current?
- How do you spend your day?
- How much time would you say you spend directly with customers and prospects?
  - What specifically do you do with them?
  - What keeps you from spending more time with them?
  - What are you working on now?

Leadership
- Tell me about a time you led a team or group of people.
  - What were the challenges you faced?
  - How did you handle those challenges?
- If someone on your team was not performing up to expectations, how would you handle it?
  - How would you help them?
- How do you earn the respect of your team and coworkers?

Passion for Sales
- Why did you choose to work in sales over another customer-facing role?
- Why are you interested in a sales position?
- How do you keep up to date on your target market?
- What core values should every sales rep have?
- How do you keep a smile on your face during a hard day?

**Adapted from <u>100 Sales Interview Questions to Ask Candidates</u> published online by HubSpot, Inc. (https://www.hubspot.com/resources/sales-hiring).

IV – Ideal Customer Profile

Demographics

- Industry/market – Industries or markets where your company competes successfully. Or, markets you have targeted to penetrate.

- Size – Company must be large enough to afford your products/ services or small enough to value the relationship you offer.

- Revenue

- Number of employees

- Location/geography/region – Geographies where you can support your customers effectively

- Products or services – Products or services that incorporate or make use of your products/services.

- Financial strength – Companies that have the financial strength to buy your products or services, or companies that rely on the strength of your company to build success.

- Culture/organization – Companies that would fit in with your company's culture or organization

- Competitive positioning – Companies that allow you to avoid competition or companies where your offering holds a competitive advantage.

Mindset

- Companies that have a pain point that your product/service will address

- Companies that are aware of their pain point or that will be receptive to your sales team making them aware of their pain point.

Relationship

- Companies where you have existing relationships or where you can quickly develop relationships

- Companies where you know current or past management or employees

- Companies that use the same vendors as your current customers

- Companies that compete with you current customers

- Companies that are currently customer of your competitors

- Companies that are in markets you currently sell to

V – Sample Commission Schedule

The company that used this commission schedule had four goals:

- Find and close new accounts

- Grow existing accounts

- Work with channel partners

- Maintain existing business

The design directs the sales rep to find and close new business accounts by paying a higher commission rate on new business. It also pays incentives to the sales rep that closes new business in existing accounts and it pays on business closed as a result of referrals form channel partners. Finally, the commission plan sets a quota for recurring business (residual sales) from existing accounts and pays on the recurring business provided the sales rep meets or exceeds quota.

Keep in mind that this is only an example of how a commission plan may be designed. Yours may be quite different since it should be tied to your business goals.

Base Salary

$XX,XXX per month

Commissions – New Sales

Company pays Commissions as a percentage of the net revenue of all new monthly sales. Net revenue equals gross revenue less discounts, returns and other customer credits. The percentage paid is based on account type or product sold as shown below.

Level	Description	Rate
Tier 1	New account, not previously known to Company	4.5%
Tier 2	New account, prospect in Company database	2.5%
Tier 3	Existing Company account	1.5%
Tier 4	Referral from channel partner	1.0%

Commissions – Residual Sales

Description	Rate
Residual sales	2.0%

Residual sales are service contracts, leases or other transactions in which the customer contracts with Company to provide a product, service or solution in return for monthly, quarterly or other regular payments. Residual sales commissions will be paid quarterly based on the previous quarter's total account revenue. Residual sales commissions are payable only if the Sales Rep attains at least 75% of assigned new sales quota in each month of the previous quarter.

VI – Strategic Plan Review – Questions to Ask

Products

- Are we meeting or exceeding targeted unit volumes, revenue and mix?

- Does product demand still meet company expectations?

- Do the products meet market and customer needs?

- Are the development schedules and product availability still viable?

- What is the competitive environment for our products?

- What competitive threats are present or visible?

- What needs to be done to address competitive threats?

Key Customers

- Are our key accounts delivering the revenue and product volumes that we have targeted?

- What does the key account sales pipeline look like for the next three, six and twelve months?

- What is the customer satisfaction level of our key accounts?

- Is our plan to penetrate our key accounts more broadly on track in terms of: new executive contacts, business units, user groups?

- What is our competitive position within our key accounts?

- Do our key accounts have additional business needs that we can or should address?

New Customers

- Have we met or exceeded our year-to-date "new account" targets for revenue and number of accounts?

- How many new accounts are in the sales pipeline?

- Where in the sales cycle are the pipeline new account prospects?

- How does our new account prospecting activity compare with our metrics?

- What is our win/loss ratio for new account opportunities?

- Do our product offerings and messaging resonate with prospects?

- Are we meeting a customer need?

Target Markets

- What is our target market penetration?

- How does our current penetration compare with where it was at the start of the plan period?

- How many of our new accounts are in our target markets?

- What does our sales pipeline look like for our target markets?

- What is our competitive position in our target markets?

- Does our product or solution offering meet the needs of our target markets?

Goals

- Are the strategic goals still valid and attainable?

- Have market conditions changed that should prompt us to change the goals, for better or worse?

Metrics

- What do our metrics tell us about our progress toward achieving our goals?

- Are we using the right metrics?

- Do we need to adjust our metrics to better measure progress or drive activity?

Commitments to Short-Term Targets

- What short-term commitments should we make to drive progress against our strategic goals?

- Who will be accountable for keeping those commitments?

Status of Previous Commitments

- What is the completion status of short-term commitments made at the last strategic plan review?

- What were the results of meeting those commitments?

Other Leading Indicators

- What do other leading indicators of success or failure tell us about our plan progress?

VII – Management Meetings Slide

WIGs, or Wildly Important Goals, is a term coined by McChesney, Covey and Huling in their book <u>The 4 Disciplines of Execution</u>, published by Free Press and copyrighted by FranklinCovey, 2012.

Acknowledgements

Thank you to my wife and editor, Marianne, for encouraging me to write this book. Her tireless patience and ability to make what was obvious to me clear to my readers were essential to making this project a success.

Thank you also to my sister Carol Wallace, an experienced public relations professional for reading the next-to-last draft of the book. Her comments and enthusiasm affirmed for me that this endeavor would prove engaging to my readers.

Index

About the Author

David Wallace's personal qualities of insight, vision, problem solving, tact, diplomacy, and leadership have made him a valued business partner for over 30 years. He is an innovative leader who brings years of entrepreneurial experience, gained from starting multiple businesses and running others. He excels in developing sales organizations (strategy, tools, people), growing the enterprise, and leading the organization to profitability. David is adept at the most critical aspects of a sales organization: setting vision and direction, creating focused strategies, communicating clearly and persuasively, developing/mentoring high-performance people, and creating long-term relationships. He is noted for setting aggressive objectives, developing/implementing strategy, leading plan development, and motivating strong teams to meet milestones.

David began his career at IBM, selling multimillion-dollar computer systems to public- and private-sector accounts, including the City of New York, Metropolitan Transportation Authority, and Merrill Lynch. Following IBM, Dave led GE Capital Computer Leasing's western sales region, delivering $140 million in annual computer lease origination, implementing sales management systems, and creating an innovative telesales organization. He also held leadership positions at several smaller companies, turning around a computer education and training company, building sales/marketing functions for a leading turbine generator maintenance provider and leading the growth of a manufacturer of high-speed coin counting and sorting machines.

To any endeavor, David brings the ability to develop high-functioning teams that deliver sales results, grow the business, and share a common vision.

David earned his MBA from Columbia University with marketing and finance concentrations, and has a B.A. in economics with a computer science minor from Georgetown University. He is active in community, educational, and professional organizations.

About Wallace Management Group

Wallace Management Group helps clients grow their businesses by specializing in three areas: strategy, sales management and marketing management.

- **Strategy** – We help clients assess their markets, customers and products. Review client company's strengths and weaknesses. We put together a strategy that works and then work with our client to implement it.

- **Sales Management** – We work with clients to provide their teams with the tools they need to meet and surpass their goals. Tools include:

  - Sales Scorecard – We conduct a 2-day defined assessment of client's sales organization and deliver recommendations to improve sales effectiveness.

  - Sales strategy

  - Territory planning

  - Incentive compensation plans

  - CRM systems and more

- **Marketing Management** – We work with clients to build the marketing programs their teams need to be successful. We help: build brands; create crisp, clear messages; and generate leads. We lead our clients to build the marketing programs they need to be sales powerhouses!

Wallace Management Group is in southwestern Connecticut, within easy reach of New York City, Boston, and all New York airports. Reach us at: www.wallacemanagement.com.

www.ingramcontent.com/pod-product-compliance
Lightning Source LLC
Chambersburg PA
CBHW070349200326
41518CB00012B/2181